The Way to Heaven

The Way to Heaven

Catechisms and Sermons in the Establishment of the Dutch Reformed Church in the East Indies

Yudha Thianto

WIPF & STOCK · Eugene, Oregon

THE WAY TO HEAVEN
Catechisms and Sermons in the Establishment of the Dutch Reformed Church in the East Indies

Copyright © 2014 Yudha Thianto. All rights reserved. Except for brief quotations in critical publications or reviews, no part of this book may be reproduced in any manner without prior written permission from the publisher. Write: Permissions, Wipf and Stock Publishers, 199 W. 8th Ave., Suite 3, Eugene, OR 97401.

Wipf & Stock
An imprint of Wipf and Stock Publishers
199 W. 8th Ave., Suite 3
Eugene, OR 97401

www.wipfandstock.com

ISBN 13: 978-1-62564-162-5

Manufactured in the U.S.A.

Contents

Acknowledgments | vii

Introduction | 1

1 The Place of Catechism in the Transplantation of Calvinism in the East Indies | 17

2 The Sermons of Wiltens and Danckaerts as Tools for the Early Establishment of Calvinism in the East Indies | 47

3 The Sermons of Franchois Caron as Further Reinforcement of the Establishment of Calvinism in the East Indies | 69

4 Intersection of Doctrine and Christian Conducts in Caron's Sermons on the Ten Commandments and the Lord's Prayer | 110

5 Transfer of Reformed Religious Concepts in the East Indies | 134

Conclusion | 156

Bibliography | 161

Acknowledgments

I STARTED THIS PROJECT following the encouragement of Prof. Richard Muller, my Doktorvater from Calvin Theological Seminary. I presented a paper on Calvin's impact on the theology and ecclesiastical practices of Reformed churches in Java, Indonesia, at the Calvin Studies Society Colloquium (CSSC) in 2009, and after the presentation Prof. Muller strongly stated that I was a very suitable person to carry on research on this topic further, given my own background and the rarity of scholars working in this area of scholarship. I am greatly indebted to Prof. Muller for his keen observation and for pointing out to me a possibility of scholarly work that I did not see before.

Dr. Thomas van den End has been very helpful to me as I was doing my research. He provided me with valuable material without which I could not have progressed as smoothly as I have. I also appreciate his warm and friendly welcome as I visited him in his home in the Netherlands. Prof. G. J. Schutte and Dr. Fred van Lieburg from the Free University, Amsterdam, have also been helpful in pointing me toward the right direction in my research. Some libraries and librarians in the Netherlands provided significant assistance as I made my research trips there. They are: the Royal Library in the Hague, the University of Leiden Library, the Royal Netherlands Institute of Southeast Asian and Caribbean Studies (KITLV), and the Library of the University of Amsterdam.

Finally, I would like to thank Trinity Christian College for its support of my research. The college granted me a sabbatical leave in the fall of 2009 to start working on this project. Beyond the sabbatical I also received several summer research grants as well as research fellowships that enabled me to have the time to write this book.

Introduction

THE DUTCH ARRIVED IN the East Indies—now Indonesia—in their search for spices at the end of the sixteenth century. Under the leadership of Cornelis de Houtman four ships landed in Bantam (now Banten) in the northwest corner of Java in 1596.[1] Even though the Portuguese and the Spaniards had already been to the region much earlier, the Dutch were able to outshine them in gaining more power and monopoly of spice trading over the archipelago and some other parts of Asia, due to the success of the Dutch East India Company (*Verenigde Oost-Indische Compagnie*, or the VOC). While the Dutch's main intention was not to spread Christianity, particularly the Calvinistic branch of Christianity, transfer of religious ideas, beliefs and practices happened between the Dutch and the indigenous people as the Dutch made close contacts with the people of the East Indies. At the time when the Dutch pioneers ventured to the archipelago to find spices, Calvinism was just accepted as the main theological foundation of Christianity in the Dutch Republic. Therefore, it happened so naturally that Calvinism was also the type of Christianity that the Dutch brought to the East Indies.

This study focuses on the early history of the establishment of Calvinism or Reformed Protestantism in the East Indies during the earliest time when the Dutch started to establish their rules on the archipelago. Particularly, this book studies how the basic teachings of Calvinism were communicated, transplanted and taught to the indigenous people of the East Indies in the seventeenth century by way of the use of catechisms and

1. Works on the history of the Dutch East India Company often mention the arrival of de Houtman and the fleet of four ships from the Netherlands. Among other works, see: Gaastra, "Organization of the VOC," 14; Nagtegaal, *Riding the Dutch Tiger*, 16; Tuck, *East India Company*, 143. See also Loon, *Golden Book of the Dutch Navigators*, 99, and Parthesius, *Dutch Ships in Tropical Waters*, 11.

the circulation of sermons of Dutch ministers, all written in Malay. The core of this study is an analysis of the main content of Calvinism that was transplanted in the region, through these catechisms and sermons, in the midst of a changing socio-cultural, political, and religious milieu in the East Indies in the seventeenth century. This book attempts to paint a picture of the transplantation by way of looking closely the Malay translations of four catechetical materials, the *Sovrat ABC*, *De Spieghel vande Maleysche Tale*, the *Heidelberg Catechism* and *De Wegh na den Hemel*, and several sermons by three Dutch ministers, Sebastian Danckaerts, Caspar Wiltens and Franchois Caron. In this book Caron's sermons receive significant attention first of all because of the large number of printed sermons he left behind. These sermons serve as an excellent window for contemporary readers to see how Caron transplanted the basic teachings of Calvinism among Christians in the East Indies in the seventeenth century. As Caron wrote in the preface of the publication of his collection of sermons, his sermons were to be read by non-ordained church workers such as school masters and visitors of the sick in remote churches at Sunday services and other days.[2] Therefore, the sermons had the significant purpose of educating the people and transplanting a deeper understanding of Reformed Protestantism in the lives of the people. Caron's effort to provide sermons on the Apostles' Creed, the Ten Commandments and the Lord's Prayer was a clear demonstration of how he wanted to teach the people with the basic knowledge of Christianity, as was a custom within the Reformed tradition. This approach was in line with the spirit of the Reformation of the sixteenth century. As early as the time of Calvin's reformation in Geneva there was already an emphasis in the need for the people to know these three pillars of Christianity. Calvin insisted that the Genevans should be able to recite the creed and to be able to pray the Lord's Prayer in French so that they knew the basic meaning of the Creed in their own language and how to pray earnestly.

This study will demonstrate how basic tenets of Christianity and theological concepts of Calvinism—concepts that were foreign to the indigenous people in the East Indies prior to the arrival of the Dutch Calvinists—were communicated and taught to the people by the Dutch ministers and other church workers employed by the VOC. Through this study this book seeks to show how important theological concepts as well as ecclesial practices of Calvinism were transplanted in the archipelago. This book pays special attention to the earliest literature available in Malay during the earlier part of

---

2 Caron, *Voorbeeldt des openbaeren Godtsdienst bestaende*, **4 recto.

Introduction

the seventeenth century as a window to see how the early transplantation or establishment of Reformed Protestantism happened there. To that end, this book looks for certain linguistic cues in the translations and sermons, such as the use of terms and concepts that were already understood and used by the people before the arrival of the Dutch, to explain how the transfer of concept happened.

As this book will reveal, the sermons of the Dutch ministers were centered on three main pillars of Christianity, the Lord's Prayer, the Ten Commandments and the Apostles' Creed. In the tradition of Reformed Protestantism, these three pillars are also the centers of the catechisms. Thus, the sermons that are based on these pillars functioned as further reinforcement of the back bone upon which basic teachings of Christianity stand. In the context of the transplantation and establishment of Reformed Protestantism, publications of the Malay translations of the catechisms and circulation of sermons written by ordained ministers took primacy over against the translation of the Bible into Malay. The complete Bible was only translated into Malay in the early eighteenth century, more than a century after the first arrival of the Dutch in the East Indies. This fact alone informs us that for the Dutch, the transfer of religious knowledge by way of catechisms and sermons was deemed more important than translating the Bible for the people so that they could read it in their native language. Thus, it shows the contemporary readers that for the Dutch in the early seventeenth century, knowledge of theological doctrines was more important than knowledge of the Bible.

This book is a work in historical theology. It focuses its study on the content of Calvinism that was brought and transplanted from its origin in Europe to a new land in Southeast Asia. While this transplantation happened in the context of colonization, and there are sections in this book that deal with the history of Dutch colonization in the East Indies, this book does not intend to provide a comprehensive history of Western colonization in the archipelago. At the same time, readers will also see that this book touches on the history of missions. The establishment of the Reformed church in the East Indies was a result of the works of the Dutch ministers and other church workers such as school teachers (or the *schoolmeesters*) and comforters of the sick (or the *ziekentroosters*) in the land,[3] and hence

---

3. This book uses the term "church workers" to refer to the school teachers and comforters of the sick who worked for the VOC in the East Indies to teach and lead worship throughout the region.

one can refer to their work as work in missions. It is certainly true that the Dutch ministers who were sent to the East Indies were not missionaries in the purest sense of the word. On this point Karl Steenbrink remarks that, while in certain areas in which the VOC had its grip there were intentional missionary efforts, the work of Dutch ministers in the East Indies focused mostly on the care of Christians, the majority of whom were Europeans, with a small number of Asians.[4] However, because of the work of these church workers, many indigenous people in the East Indies came into contact with Reformed Protestantism. Therefore, as this book studies the establishment of the Reformed church in the East Indies, it also shows how the gospel was spread to that part of Southeast Asia through the efforts of these church workers.

In recent years, some historians have shown interests in the history of the VOC in the seventeenth and eighteenth centuries. More particularly, studies on various aspects of life in Batavia as the center of the VOC's operation have been done by Hendrik Niemeijer,[5] Jean Gelman-Taylor[6] and Leonard Blussé.[7] Other studies on the presence of the VOC in the East Indies have also been done by various historians such as Luc Nagtegaal[8] and G. J. Schutte.[9] Scholarly works that focus on the early history of the Calvinist church in the East Indies at the time of the VOC, however, are more rare. G. J. Schutte may be seen as the champion who has worked extensively on the topic.[10] Some other scholars have also worked on larger aspects of the early history of Reformed Protestantism in the archipelago.[11] These works, however, mostly focus on the perspectives of the Dutch ministers and the Dutch experience in the East Indies. In the Indonesian language, Thomas van den End has made a significant contribution in the study of the history of the church in Indonesia. His two-volume work entitled *Ragi Carita*

---

4. Steenbrink, "Arrival of Protestantism and the Consolidation of Christianity," 99.
5. Niemeijer, *Calvinisme en koloniale stadscultuur*.
6. Taylor, *Social World of Batavia* and also *Indonesia: Peoples and Histories*.
7. Blussé, *Strange Company*
8. Nagtegaal, *Riding the Dutch Tiger*.
9. Among other works, see Schutte, *State and Trade in the Indonesian Archipelago*.
10. Schutte, *Het Indisch Sion*.
11. There is only a small number of scholarly works devoted to this particular topic, such as: De Jong, "Early Reformed Missions in the East Indies," and Aritonang and Steenbrink, *History of Christianity in Indonesia*.

Introduction

is still widely used in several seminaries in Indonesia as the best general introduction to Indonesian church history.[12]

This book takes a slightly different focus than the above-mentioned works on the history of the church in the East Indies at the time of the VOC. As it closely studies the Malay texts available to the indigenous people then, it will present the history of the expansion of Calvinism in the East Indies on the level of the people who received it, and on the grounds where it was transplanted. By primarily looking at the Malay texts this book attempts to demonstrate how Calvinism started to take its roots among the indigenous people. These Malay texts reveal the content of Reformed Protestantism that the Dutch wanted to communicate to the indigenous people. Since language is the most important element in communication, looking at the process of transplantation by way of the use of the language of the target group is a necessary step in understanding the process. The way the catechisms were translated into Malay gives contemporary readers an opportunity to see the process of communication between the Dutch ministers and the people in the East Indies. The presence of these Malay texts was a clear indication that the Dutch ministers took their job of teaching new converts the basic beliefs of Calvinism very seriously. While it was really the case that most—if not all—indigenous people in the East Indies spoke their own regional languages other than Malay as their mother tongue, to a certain extent the people knew Malay. The language had been a *lingua franca* for quite some time before the first arrival of the Dutch. As readers will see in this book, the multiple publications of these Malay texts throughout the seventeenth century is a good indicator that these Malay texts were needed and the native people understood Malay. In so doing this book explores the translatability and applicability of theological doctrines to show their universality, and at the same time this book also seeks to explain the need for contextualization of these doctrines in their translation and application. This process became very interesting as the transplantation crossed cultural, ethnic and linguistic boundaries. In this book readers will see that the transplantation was rooted in a strong and faithful adherence to the source—namely Calvinism as it was held and interpreted by the Reformed

---

12. End, *Ragi Carita*. Moreover, van den End has made very large contributions to the study of the Indonesian church history through his many works that look particular areas in Indonesia, such as: *De Nederlandse Zendingsvereniging in West-Java, Sumber-Sumber Zending tentang Sejarah Gereja Toraja, Sumber-Sumber Zending tentang Sejarah Gereja Kristen Sumba, Enam Belas Dokumen Dasar Calvinisme* and many other works published in Dutch, Indonesian and English.

church in the Netherlands—but at the same time the ministers and church workers that did the work were also very sensitive to the immediate situation among the natives of the East Indies. At times, as illustrated by the issue of baptisms of children of slaves discussed in this book, and also as the ecclesiastical decisions and the correspondence between the ministers in the East Indies and the Netherlands demonstrate, this attempt at contextualization created tensions. Such tensions were partly caused by the effort to maintain orthodoxy, and partly caused by political and economic interests of the VOC and the Dutch government. But in the end the process of transplantation continued and the new church being formed in the East Indies became established, bearing similar colors as the one in the Netherlands, but also having its own overtones as a Calvinist church in the East.

As this book unfolds, it will further provide readers with a fresher understanding of the history of expansion of Calvinism in the East Indies under the power and care of the VOC. This book, then, demonstrates the contextualization that happened when Calvinism was introduced in the East Indies in the early seventeenth century. As the study provides an in-depth look at the way Calvinism was made accessible to the indigenous people in the East Indies, it unveils the intercommunication between the Dutch- and the Malay-speaking people. In order for the Dutch ministers to effectively bring the teaching of Reformed Protestantism to the people, they had to be able to contextualize their message to their audience. The Malay translations of the catechisms together with the sermons provide a framework for us to see how the theology and concepts of Calvinism were explained. By analyzing the way the translators and ministers used Malay terms, words and phrases to represent and explain key theological terms, this book will illustrate what kind of accommodation and contextualization these translators and ministers made in order for the people to understand the content of Reformed Christianity.

Even though in a large portion the transplantation of Reformed Protestantism in the East Indies was done the Western way, and the new converts to Christianity did have to learn the content, the way of worship and the rites of Western Christianity, this study will show that contextualization is unavoidable when concepts are communicated and transferred to other cultures. The ministers and translators used words and concepts that were readily available to the indigenous people. This book further demonstrates the fact that translation is, to a certain measure, interpretation. In order to be able to communicate the theological concepts within Calvinism from the source language to the target language, the translators and preachers had to know what the people already knew, and the communication of the concepts involved interpretation in the form of contextualization of the concepts. As the Portuguese had arrived in the archipelago a few decades before the Dutch, the Portuguese language had been assimilated into Malay. On matters pertaining to religion, several Portuguese terms and expressions had been used by the people who became Catholics through the works of the Jesuit missionaries who came to the land. The contextualization of Calvinism in the archipelago, therefore, included the adoption and adaptation of those Portuguese words and terms into the discourse that the Dutch Calvinists introduced to the people.

This book consistently uses the term "East Indies" to refer to the region over which the VOC had its authority starting from the early years of the seventeenth century to its dissolution in 1799. Even though the majority of the area later became the country of Indonesia, calling the region "Indonesia" when dealing with the seventeenth century is anachronistic. While it tries to provide a clearer picture of how the transplantation happened throughout the entire archipelago, often times this book concentrates more on Ambon and Batavia as VOC centers of operation. The forts in Batavia and Ambon were central in the VOC's operations, and naturally the two places also became central in the church's work. Ministers from the Netherlands were first sent to these two places before they were commissioned to minister and serve other regions throughout the archipelago.

The title of this book, *The Way to Heaven*, is the English translation of the Dutch title of the small catechism of Spiljardus, later also published by Franchois Caron under the title *De Wegh na Den Hemel*, which is one of the catechetical materials studied in this book. This title best reflects the fundamental belief held by the Reformed church in the Netherlands, and formed the core of the belief of the ministers and church workers who labored in the East Indies. They strongly believed that Calvinism or Reformed Protestantism is the only way to heaven. Over against Islam and other pagan religions that already had very strong grips in the archipelago even before they came, these Reformed believers stood proudly in proclaiming that the only way to salvation, and thus to heaven, is by following exactly what they teach and proclaim. For them belief in Jesus Christ as explained by the doctrines of Calvinism is the only way to heaven. Over against Roman Catholicism brought by the Jesuit missionaries and the Portuguese—their sworn enemies and competitors—the Dutch strongly believed that Calvinism is the only true religion that can bring eternal salvation. Following the commonly held conviction of the Reformed believers of the sixteenth and seventeenth centuries, they considered Roman Catholicism a false religion. In a very prominent way, in their insistence that the Reformed faith is the only way to heaven, these ministers and church workers advanced the message conveyed by the first question and answer of the Heidelberg Catechism, that our only comfort in life and in death is that we belong, body and soul, to our faithful savior Jesus Christ.

The earliest transplantation of Calvinism in the archipelago happened as the Dutch East India Company started to establish its stronghold in most of the Southeast Asian region. The Dutch East East India Company (VOC) was officially created in 1602.[13] The foundation of the VOC was spelled out in the charter, or *Octrooi van de Verenigde Oostindische Compagnie*.[14] The charter was granted by the States-General. The 1602 *Octrooi* did not have a particular article that was directly related to religion. However, given the way the VOC operated in the East Indies, and the different ways the VOC related to different sultanates and regions in the archipelago, as well as interactions with the Poruguese who were already there before the arrival of the Dutch, the VOC had to deal with matters concerning religion. The early days of the VOC happened during the time when the Netherlands was embracing the teaching of the Reformation, particularly the Calvinist branch. The end of the sixteenth century saw the Low Countries becoming Reformed in their theological outlook. The birth of the Belgic Confession in 1561 was one important milestone indicating the strength of the influence of the Calvinist Reformed church in that part of Europe. Written by Guide de Bres, the Belgic Confession was adopted by the Reformed Synod at Emden in 1571 and then reaffirmed by the National Synod of Dordt in 1619.[15] Together with the Belgic Confession, the Heidelberg Catechism, which was approved by a synod in Heidelberg in 1563, had been accepted by the Synod of Dordt as the confessional standards of the Reformed churches in the Netherlands. When the Dutch sailed to the East Indies and the VOC was established in 1602, the two confessional standards of the Reformed church had become the main foundation of the church. Soon,

---

13. For a good, brief history of the founding of the VOC see Gaastra, "Introduction."

14. "VOC Octrooi 1602," in Valenteyn, *Ooud en Nieuw oost-Indien*, 1:96–103. Hereafter: "VOC Octroi 1602" followed by article number.

15. Schaff, *Creeds of Christendom*, 3:383.

Introduction

when worship services were conducted in the new land, the Dutch modeled church worship and teachings after that contained in these two confessional standards.

The VOC was born to unite six companies that were already in existence as soon as the first fleet of 1595–1597 had demonstrated the profit of trading in Asia.[16] The company was headed by seventeen people, who are commonly called the *Heeren XVII*.[17] The seventeen gentlemen were to come from the four chambers that formed the pre-companies (the *voorcompagnieen*), namely Amsterdam, Zeeland, Maas, North-Holland and Friesland. Because Amsterdam was the largest group, it was represented by eight gentlemen, while Zeeland was represented by four, and Maas and North-Holland were represented by two people each. The seventeenth member of the board would be nominated by Zeeland, Maas and North-Holland by a vote.[18] The VOC had sixty directors, twenty in the Amsterdam Chamber, twelve in Zeeland, and seven in each of the other chambers.[19] Even with such elaborate structrue of leadership, the organization of the VOC was not perfect. Gaastra plainly describes the central management of the company as badly constructed. He points out several issues pertaining to the bad management, with the three leading problems being the irregularity of the meeting sessions of the *Heeren XVII*, constant changes in the composition of the assembly, and lack of administrative staff for the *Heeren XVII*.[20]

Politically, in the Netherlands when the VOC was being formed, the country consisted of seven provinces and known as the *Republiek der Verenigde Nederlanden* or the Republic of the United Netherlands. These seven provinces were: Holland, Zeeland, Groningen, Friesland, Utrecht, Overijssel and Gelre. Each province was led by the *Gewestelijke Staten* or the regional governing body, and the *Gewestelijke Staten* appointed a governor or *Stadhouder* who held the military authority, with policies for the Republic decided by the States-General.[21] Each province sent its delegates to be members of the States-General. Gepken-Jager points out that talk within the States-General was often very difficult, because each delegate

---

16. Gaastra, "Foundation of the VOC," in *The Archives of the Dutch East India Company*, 14.
17. "VOC Octrooi 1602," article 2.
18. "VOC Octrooi 1602," article 3.
19. "VOC Octrooi 1602," article 25.
20. Gaastra, "Organization of the VOC," 22.
21. Gepken-Jager, "Verenigde Oost-Indische Compagnie (VOC)," 45.

had rigidly delineated tasks, and each new decision had to be taken back to the regional governing body.[22]

The VOC was also born in the time when the Netherlands was at war with Spain and Portugal, and thus, as Gaastra has stated, a united company would also be a strong weapon, militarily and economically, against these two enemies.[23] The preamble of the charter clearly stated that the VOC was formed in order to provide direction and to prescribe navigation of trading and commerce in the East Indies.[24] Enmity with Spain and Portugal rose to the foreground in the *Octrooi* in that it explicitly mentioned that should there be fights with the fleet from these two countries, the VOC's ship captain may capture the ship and the goods from the ship may be confiscated. The ship's goods could be divided up according to the country's priority, namely divided up between the country and the admiral.[25] Political struggles between the Dutch and the Iberian nations at the end of the sixteenth century carried over into the early seventeenth century. The founding of the VOC became another opportunity for the Dutch to fight against these nations far away from their homeland. In the East Indies the Dutch wanted to establish their authority not only in the area of commerce and spice trading, but also religiously. Representing the Dutch government, the VOC carried out a similar calling that the government must also maintain the practice of the true religion. In the Netherlands, religion and the state were inseparable. Functioning as a representation of the Dutch in the East Indies, the VOC advanced the interests of the Dutch government in Asia. Matters pertaining to religion were therefore deemed important by the VOC. As Calvinism had been accepted by the government in the Netherlands, it was also advanced in the Indies. Within Calvinism confessional standards had always been considered fundamental. The Belgic Confession was used as one important guide in the Calvinist churches in Europe. The confession specifies that the state must advance a society that is pleasing to God, and that civil rulers have the task to remove every obstacle that will hinder the preaching of the gospel.[26] The practical application of this teaching of the confession, in the context of early-seventeenth-century struggles between the Dutch and the Iberian nations in the East Indies, was to drive

22. Gepken-Jager, "Verenigde Oost-Indische Compagnie (VOC)," 45.
23. Gaastra, "Organization of the VOC," 14.
24. "VOC Octrooi 1602," preamble.
25. "VOC Octrooi 1602," article 37.
26. Belgic Confession, article 36.

away the Portuguese and the Spaniards as the VOC started to establish its authority in the archipelago. Thus, even though the 1602 *Octrooi* of the VOC did not explicitly spell out issues concerning religion, the political and economic struggles between the Dutch and the Iberian nations (especially with Portugal) and the impact of the Dutch's hold of the Belgic Confession as their confessional document brought the VOC into the issues of religion.

The Iberian enemies of the Dutch, most importantly the Portuguese, had been in the Indies several decades before the arrival of the Dutch. With the Portuguese came Roman Catholicism. Jesuit missionaries came to Ambon and the surrounding islands in the southern part of the Moluccas in the middle of the sixteenth century. Portuguese merchants who came to the Moluccas Islands, especially to Ambon and Ternate, in the early 1530s to trade spices with the native Moluccans also tried to convert the people to Christianity. This conversion was more politically and economically motivated than for true religious conversion. Nonetheless, many native Moluccans were baptized as the result of this interaction.[27] Francis Xavier landed in Ambon in 1546 and discovered that the so-called Christians were not really living as Christians are supposed to. He right away devoted his life to the spiritual development of the people, baptizing infants and working to bring Muslims and pagans into Roman Catholicism.[28] Xavier later went to the island of Ternate, also a part of the Moluccas Islands, and he was equally successful in spreading Roman Catholicism there.[29] In Ternate Xavier developed a simple catechism in the form of poetry that contained an explanation of the Apostles' Creed. The catechism was written in Portuguese but then translated into Malay and was widely used all over the Moluccas Islands.[30] Translating religious texts into Malay was a necessary step to ensure that the indigenous people could understand the message of Christianity. Malay was already the *lingua franca* of the entire region, even though each area and even each island in the archipelago also spoke its own language and dialect.

One clear example of the fight against Roman Catholic "superstition" that the Dutch minister continually showed was on the issue of baptism. Carrying the medieval practice into the seventeenth century, the Roman Catholics allowed midwives to baptize in case of emergency. The insistence

---

27. End, *Ragi Carita*, 1:38.
28. Kelley, *Life of Saint Francis Xavier*, 143.
29. Bartoli and Maffei, *Life of St. Francis Xavier*, 219.
30. End, *Ragi Carita*, 1:49.

to baptize babies during worship services was a clear reaction against Roman Catholic baptism. Xavier emphasized the necessity of baptizing babies as soon as possible. He instructed the Jesuit missionaries to diligently visit people's houses and inquire for unbaptized babies. If he strongly instructed these missionaries, we have reasons to believe that he did the same while he was in the Moluccas. Therefore, the people on the archipelago were accustomed to seeing and hearing the Roman Catholic theology and practice of baptism. When the Reformed ministers came to the islands, they had to transplant the Reformed understanding of baptism that was different from that of the Roman Catholics.[31]

For the Dutch, faithfulness to the Belgic Confession also meant driving away the Portuguese along with the "superstition" of Roman Catholicism that they carried. Therefore, the VOC's economic and political interests were also accompanied by a religious overtone. The fight against the Portuguese did not just mean economic gains for the glory of the Dutch Republic and the wealth of the people; it also meant faithfulness to their church. Thus, ever since the earliest time of the VOC the Dutch had always brought with them zeal to establish the foundations of Calvinism in the archipelago, as an expression of their religious beliefs as well as a demonstration of their superiority over the Portuguese. What followed was that as the Dutch planted stronger roots of Calvinism, struggles against the Portuguese and Roman Catholicism kept appearing. Later on the ministers who preached in Malay to the indigenous people of the Indies often engaged themselves in certain forms of polemics against Roman Catholicism. However, at the same time, given the fact that the Portuguese and Roman Catholicism had been present in the archipelago several decades before the arrival of the Dutch, Portuguese language and certain concepts of Christianity that were already taught by the Jesuit missionaries to the indigenous people remained. Thus, the Dutch ministers who preached to the people and the translations of catechisms and other Protestant printed material had to borrow from the Portuguese and Roman Catholic vocabularies. Therefore, the Dutch were also indebted to the Portuguese, as far as the transplantation of Calvinism went.

The Dutch worked fast in bringing Reformed Protestantism into the East Indies. In 1611, only nine years after the VOC charter was written, a

---

31. Xavier, "To the Fathers of the Society of Jesus Working among the Christians of the Comorin Coast," letter 59, February 1548, in Coleridge, *Life and Letters of St. Francis Xavier*, 2:24.

Introduction

small catechism book intended to provide learning instruction for young children was published in Malay. This book, published in Amsterdam and believed to have been put together by Albert Ruyl, is entiled *Sovrat ABC*.[32] It was clearly intended to lay down a basic foundation of Reformed Christianity for the indigenous children. The publication of this small book in a very large measure demonstrates that the Dutch wanted to establish a strong root of knowledge of the content of Reformed Christianity. The keenness of the Dutch to provide this religious instruction in Malay is also commendable. The East Indies archipelago is a vast chain of thousands of islands on the equator inhabited by varied ethnic groups with their distinct languages. The diversity of the people was enormous. However, even with hundreds of distinct languages spoken by these people, Malay had become a *lingua franca* of most of the people in the archipelago long before the arrival of the Dutch. While there were still difficulties with regard to the use of language, publishing works in Malay, and later on preaching in Malay, was the best approach the Dutch ministers could have to bring Reformed Christianity to the people. The Dutch's effort to learn Malay and to be able to communicate in Malay was the first most important step in communication with the people. The publication of the *Sovrat ABC* in Malay in 1611 is the most valuable demonstration. There was already a strong effort in the publication of this work to bring Protestantism to the Malay-speaking people, especially to children. This small book included the Malay translations of the Ten Commandments, the Lord's Prayer, the Apostles' Creed and several standard prayers.[33]

Very early in its presence in the archipelago, the VOC published a Malay dictionary, compiled by Frederick de Houtman, who later became the first VOC governor of Ambon (1605–1611). The dictionary was entitled *Spraeck ende woord-boeck, In de Maleysche ende Madagaskarsche Talen, metes vele Arabische ende Tursche woorden*, and was published in Amsterdam in 1603.[34] The fact that this book was published only a year after the VOC charter was written demonstrates the willingness of the Dutch leaders to know Malay. The dictionary underwent several reprints and the Dutch-Malay portion of the dictionary was included in Albert Ruyl's *Spieghel vande maleysche Tale*.[35] In this edition, the dictionary was attached in the back

32. Ruyl, *Sovrat ABC*.
33. See the discussion on the book in the following chapter.
34. See Landwehr, *VOC*, no. 748.
35. Ruyl, *Spieghel vande Maleysche Tale*, A1 recto–K4 recto, back part. I am indebted

part of the book, with a new collation. According to William Marsden, the dictionary was republished under different title, *Dictionarium, ofte woord end spraeck boeck in de Duytsche ende Maleytsche Tale*, in 1673 and again in Batavia in 1707, and in English it was published under the title *Dialogus in the English and Malaiane Languages* in London in 1614.[36] The subsequent reprints of the dictionary signify its importance in the VOC's dealings with the indigenous people in the East Indies. As the Dutch continued to fight the Portuguese politically, commercially and religiously, the mastery of Malay was a must for them. In order to gain more hold on the indigenous people, the Dutch had to be able to undo the influence of the Portuguese. Since the Portuguese had already had the advantage of translating certain basic teachings of Christianity, such as the Apostles' Creed and the Lord's Prayer, into Malay, the Dutch had to do the same and then surpass them.

Since the earliest time when the Dutch sailed far into the Indies, there were already individuals who had the desire to bring Calvinism into this foreign land. The VOC, however, was first and foremost founded as a trading company and thus it did not see evangelization as its main task. However, since the Dutch who sailed to the Indies needed spiritual guidance and needed to worship in a church setting familiar to them, the VOC had the responsibility to provide such worship environment for the people. Van den End has reported that on the issue of evangelization, the VOC was not at first interested in bringing the indigenous people to become Christians. But as the strength of the company grew, and when it saw that in certain areas of the Indies converting the people to be Protestant meant gaining more loyal supporters of the company, it started to be more and more interested in bringing these people into the church. Most preachers, according to Van den End, would remain in the forts, and there were not many preachers who would leave the forts to evangelize to the people living in remote places. Within the confines of the forts the ministers were taken care of by the VOC. Van den End has also noticed that as the number of Christians in the East Indies grew, the VOC remained a strong force in steering the course and development of Christianity there. The churches in the Indies must follow the worship style and the church order of the Reformed church in

---

to Dr. van den End for pointing out that the dictionary in Ruyl's *Spieghel* is in fact taken from de Houtman's *Sprack end Woord-Boeck*.

36. Marsden, *Grammar of the Malayan Language*, xxxviii–xxxix.

the Netherlands. At the same time, the church leaders had to be sent from the Netherlands and these church leaders were employed by the VOC.[37]

The VOC employed *ziekentrooster* or comforters of the sick to accompany the Dutch who sailed to the East Indies to provide comfort for those who were on the ship. But more than just taking care of the sick people, they also provided some spiritual leadership to the people. Often the comforters of the sick also performed the duties that would normally be done by ordained ministers. Philippus Pieterszoon is a good example of such comforter of the sick. He came from Delft and in 1598 he went to Mauritius and preached there twice. Then he went to Madagaskar and baptized a slave. Van Troostenburg de Bruijn notes that Piterszoon was called a *predikant*, or preacher.[38] However, de Bruijn recognizes that Pieterszoon was not strictly a preacher or ordained minister who had the right to preach, but only a comforter of the sick. However, even though he was not an ordained preacher, he had a mandate that allowed him to baptize.[39] De Bruijn also notes that even though Pieterszoon was often praised as a stern and fearless "preacher," he was not a good comforter of the sick.[40] The case of Pieterszoon is a good example of how the task of a comforter of the sick became confused with that of a preacher or minister. Because in the earlier time of the voyage from the Netherlands to the Indies there was a scarcity of ordained ministers to sail to the new land, comforters of the sick had to step in. This was a problem for the Reformed church in the Netherlands that placed significant emphasis on proper maintenance of church offices.

The first ordained minister to come to the East Indies was Caspar Wiltens. He was originally from Antwerp and was sent by the classis of Walcheren to minister in Ambon from 1615 to 1625.[41] Before he eventually stayed in Ambon, he ministered on the islands of Bachian (or Bachan) and Machian in the Moluccas in 1612 and then in Banda in 1614. Wiltens was the only preacher in Ambon until 1618 or 1619, and later a colleague, Sebastian Danckaerts, joined him there.[42] Together Wiltens and Danckaerts ministered to the people in Ambon and the surrounding islands for many years. Their experience is a good illustration of how challenging the minis-

---

37. End, *Ragi Carita*, 1:34.
38. Bruijn, *Hervormde Kerk in Nederlandsch Oost-Indie*, 5.
39. See also Bruijn, *Biographisch Woordenboek van Oost-Indische Predikanten*, 338.
40. Bruijn, *Hervormde Kerk*, 6.
41. Bruijn, *Hervormde Kerk*, 7.
42. Bruijn, *Bigraphisch Woordenboek*, 488.

terial situation in the Indies was. The scarcity of ordained ministers on the islands hindered effective ecclesial works.

Wiltens and Danckaerts, as also Caron and other ministers who labored in some parts of the Dutch East Indies, were very much aware that they were competing against Roman Catholicism and other religions that had taken a foothold in the archipelago long before the arrival of the Dutch. It was their firm belief in the supremacy of Calvinism that carried them in their labor of spreading the teaching of this particular branch of Christianity. Over against the politics of the VOC, they believed that Calvinism is the only way to bring people to heaven. Other religions may attempt to teach people what heaven may look like, but the truth of Calvinism would be the one that would win the day. Through the Malay translations of the catechisms and circulated sermons that we study in this book, contemporary readers will see that these works are testimonies of what these ministers believed. At the same time these documents also provide a glimpse of how this branch of Protestantism was transplanted in the East Indies.

1

The Place of Catechism in the Transplantation of Calvinism in the East Indies

Sovrat ABC as the Earliest Reformed Catechetical Material in the East Indies

In 1611 the VOC published a small primer intended to be used in schools to teach children in the East Indies how to read and write. The title of this printed material is: *Sovrat ABC, Akan meng ayd jer anack boudack sepercy deayd 'jern 'ja capada segala manusia Nassarany: daen berbagy sombahayang Christiaan.*[1] In English, this title means, "ABC Letter, Intended to Teach Young Children the Same Material Intended for All Christians, and Some Christian Prayers." As the title page indicates, this primer was to be used to provide the basic teachings of Christianity. The title page also indicates that the content of this little book is the same as the content of the teaching of the Christian faith taught to Christians in different parts of the world. Even though this little book was published by the Dutch whose theological standpoint was Calvinism, the book still claims that the content of its teaching is universal. Even though this primer was not written in a format of questions and answers commonly used in a more formal catechism such as the Heidelberg Catechism, it fits within the genre of catechism, for, as Robert Bast claims, beginning from

---

1. Ruyl, *Sovrat ABC*.

the sixteenth century the term "catechism" was used as "a technical term for a genre of didactic religious literature."[2]

The book does not mention the name of the author. John Landwehr attributes the book to Albert Ruyl.[3] There is no dedicatory epistle accompanying the publication of this small book. Landwehr's attribution of this work to Ruyl is based on the forewords that Ruyl wrote in the publication of another catechetical work published 1612, the Malay translation of Philip van Marnix's small catechism that Ruyl translated into Malay as *Spieghel van de Maleysche Tale*.[4] In the foreword of the *Spieghel* Ruyl mentions that in the year preceding the publication of this book, he had translated another work by van Marnix entitled "A. B Boek" from low Dutch into Malay.[5] Considering that the *Spieghel* was translated in 1612, and the other smaller catechism book was published in 1611 with the main title *Sovrat ABC*, we can be certain that this small work was also translated by Ruyl.

The *Sovrat ABC* was published, first of all, to teach young children to read and write. This primer starts with a list of the alphabet printed in several different fonts. There are seven kinds of fonts included in the first page of this book, either in lower case or upper case.[6] This list of the alphabet was very likely intended to teach school children to learn their ABCs, as the title of the whole work indicates. The next part of the book is dedicated to the study of vowels and the combination of vowels and consonants. Following the lesson on the alphabet, the *Sovrat ABC* has the Malay translation of the Ten Commandments.[7] The title given to this section is *Sabda Allah ta-Allah jang Sapoulo Percara*, or "The Words of God of All Gods in Ten Items." This Malay translation of the title Ten Commandments may sound cumbersome when translated into modern English, however, for the indigenous people in the East Indies in the early years of the seventeenth century, this rather long title was necessary to teach them what the Ten Commandments actually are. It seems that Ruyl was trying to show the people that these words are God's words. In addition, the name *Allah ta-allah*, or "God of All Gods," indicates that Ruyl was setting Reformed Christianity against other religions. Thus, Ruyl indirectly showed that Reformed Christianity is the

2. Bast, *Honor Your Father*, xvii.
3. Landwehr, *VOC*, 662.
4. Ruyl, *Spieghel van de Maleysche Tale*.
5. Ruyl, *Spieghel van de Maleysche Tale*, A2 recto.
6. Ruyl, *Sovrat ABC*, A2 recto.
7. Ruyl, *Sovrat ABC*, A3 recto–A4 recto.

The Place of Catechism in the Transplantation of Calvinism in the East Indies

only true religion. The inclusion of the Ten Commandments as the first text in this small catechetical material intended as teaching material for young children gives us the impression that Ruyl considered the Ten Commandments as the most important text that children as well as adults of the East Indies must know.

Ruyl included the biblical reference to this text. "Exodus 20" is printed underneath the main title. It is worth noting here that at the time when the *Sovrat ABC* was first published, the people in the East Indies still did not have the Bible in their vernacular. The first Malay translation of the Gospel of Matthew, also done by Ruyl, was published in 1629.[8] The entire Old and New Testament Bible was only published in Malay more than a century later, in 1733.[9] Because the complete Bible was only translated into Malay at a much later time, we can consider the printing of the text of the Ten Commandments, including the Bible reference of Exodus 20, as the earliest printing of a biblical text in Malay for the people.

The placing of the Ten Commandments as the first religious instruction in the *Sovrat ABC* fits within the overall program of the Protestant Reformation in the sixteenth century. As Bast's work has shown us, the sixteenth-century Reformers followed their medieval predecessors in using the Ten Commandments as a basic instruction in faith and morality.[10] The earliest Dutch ministers who went to the East Indies followed their sixteenth-century predecessors in advancing the same idea. The Ten Commandments should be taught to the little children in the East Indies, in the language that they could easily understand, so that they too could receive basic instruction in faith and morality.

Following the text of the Ten Commandments, the *Sovrat ABC* has the text of the Apostles' Creed.[11] The title given to the creed in Malay is *Segala bagy capalang dary agama heakiman Christan*, meaning "All Headings of the Belief of the Christian Religion." Ruyl did not use the term "Apostles' Creed" perhaps for the reason that it would confuse the people. What the people needed was to know the content of the creed, the statement of their faith. The Malay term *capalang* or sometimes *capala* means "head." In the

---

8. Ruyl, *Het Nieuwe testament*.

9. 'Elkitab, 'ija 'itu segala surat Perdjanji'an Lama dan Baruw. Atas Titah segala Tuwan Pemarentah Kompanija tersalin kepada bahasa Malajuw (Amsterdam: R. and Dj. Wet'istejn, 1733).

10. Bast, *Honor Your Fathers*, 1–2.

11. Ruyl, *Sovrat ABC*, A4 recto–verso.

vocabulary list that Ruyl included at the end of his *Spieghel*, he clearly states that the word *capala* is the synonym for the Dutch word *hooft*.[12] Thus, the Malay title for the Apostle's Creed is to communicate that these twelve articles are to be understood as the head or the most important points of the beliefs of the Christian religion. In the title Ruyl used, the Malay word *heakiman* was the synonym for the Dutch word *ghelooven* in the vocabulary list at the end of the *Spieghel*.[13] In the translation of the Apostles' Creed Ruyl used the first-person singular pronoun *hamba* to translate "I." The word *hamba* in Malay has the connotation of humility. Literally the word means a lowly servant or even a slave. Thus, in the catechism, this word also shows the humility of the person in the presence of God. Ruyl must have rendered this word suitable to express a Christian's belief as expressed in the creed.

The Malay translation of the Lord's Prayer follows the Apsotles' Creed. In this primer, the Malay title of the prayer is *Sombahayang tuankoe Iesu Christi*.[14] In English, the title means, "The Prayer of My Lord Jesus Christ." The Malay word *somba*, which is the root word of *sombahayang*, means to worship or give the highest respect to somebody else. In the vocabulary list that Ruyl included in the *Spieghel*, the word is used as a synonym for *ghebeden*.[15] The term *tuankoe* means "my Lord." The title thus reflects the overall meaning of the Lord's Prayer as the prayer that was taught by the Lord Jesus Christ. At the same time, by using the first-person singular possessive pronoun "my," there is a sense that Ruyl was bringing the prayer into a more personal experience of the people instead of the communal praying experience. Ruyl moved away from the common custom of looking at the prayer as a communal prayer and using the plural possessive pronoun "our." This translation shows a departure from the custom of the churches of the day. Even in the Dutch language, the common designation of *onze Vader* was widely used in the Netherlands.

Forms[16] for baptism and the Lord's Supper are included in this primer. The form for baptism is simple. It starts with a direct citation from Matthew 28:18–19, without explicit mention of the biblical reference. What is notable is that this form does not introduce that it was Jesus who spoke in that passage. The form merely starts with the statement: "God of all gods has

---

12. Ruyl, *Spieghel van de maleysche Tale*, D1 recto.
13. Ruyl, *Spieghel van de maleysche Tale*, C3 verso.
14. Ruyl, *Sovrat ABC*, A4 verso.
15. Ruyl, *Spieghel*, C3 verso.
16. The English "form" is used here to translate the Dutch word *formulier*.

The Place of Catechism in the Transplantation of Calvinism in the East Indies

given me all the powers in heaven and on earth, and therefore go teach all people and baptize them in the name of the Father, Son and Holy Spirit."[17] The next sentence tells the people that whoever believes and receives this baptism will be made righteous, but those who do not believe will perish, both their bodies and spirits.

The form for celebrating the Lord's Supper is as simple as the form for baptism. The institution of the Lord's Supper is done by way of briefly paraphrasing the biblical story of Jesus' Last Supper with the disciples. There is no biblical reference mentioned in this form. The institution says that "in the night before he was arrested by the Pharisees, Jesus Christ took the bread and prayed."[18] The Pharisees were singled out in this passage, perhaps to simplify the complex story of the arrest of Jesus as told in the four Gospels. It is very likely that Ruyl did not want to overburden the people in the East Indies with all the detail of the arrest, considering that they still did not have the Gospels translated into their language. What's important in this form is that the people can understand that Jesus was arrested by the people who wanted his death. Therefore, the form provides a very short, simplified historical context of the Lord's Supper. The message for the people seems to be that what is important for them to know is that Jesus was about to be arrested and he celebrated the supper with the disciples. The most important part, as the form shows, is that the celebration of the Lord's Supper is the celebration of the new covenant in his blood, and that as many times as they celebrate the supper they celebrate it in his memory.[19]

The next section in the *Sovrat ABC* explains the procedure of settling disputes among brothers and sisters as taught by Jesus in Matthew 18. This section is in fact a translation of Matthew 18:15–18.[20] The text shows that as much as possible, disputes between two brothers or sisters in the Lord should be settled privately, and each person should stand before the Lord with a clean conscience. By so doing, each party could maintain peace in the community. Therefore, the new believers could witness to the people around them that Christians can maintain peace in the community, without fights and quarrels when they have disagreement among themselves.

Texts for a morning prayer, evening prayer and prayer before meals are listed successively in the *Sovrat ABC*. There is an explicit mention that

17. Ruyl, *Sovrat ABC*, A5 recto.
18. Ruyl, *Sovrat ABC*, A5 recto.
19. Ruyl, *Sovrat ABC*, A5 recto.
20. Ruyl, *Sovrat ABC*, A5 verso.

the morning prayer is supposed to be ended with the Lord's Prayer. The prayer before meals is the Malay translation of Psalm 145:15–16, which points out that all eyes look up to God so that God will give food for all the people. This biblical passage is a good reminder that food and other blessings only come from God. However, the biblical reference is not given in the text. A quote from Luke 21:34–35 is included right after the prayer before meals. Interestingly, a reference to Luke 21 is included but without the exact verses. This passage reminds the people of Jesus' warning of the end of time, which includes his encouragement that people's hearts should not be weighed down by dissipation and drunkenness. The inclusion of this biblical passage seems a little bit out of the context in which the message of Luke is written. However, the insertion of this passage right after the prayer before meals may have been meant to remind the people to avoid drunkenness.

The prayer for after meals ends the entire book. The *Sovrat ABC* mentions the biblical text from which this prayer is taken. It states that the text is from *saboer Movsa 5.8*.[21] The Malay term *saboer* or *zabur* generally means "psalm." The *Sovrat ABC* uses this term to refer to the works of Moses. In this case, the reference to number 5 indicates that this passage is taken from the fifth book of Moses, namely Deuteronomy. The number 8 in this reference points to the eighth chapter of Deuteronomy. It is rather curious why the *Sovrat ABC* uses this way of referencing Deuteronomy. Quite likely, it is because the people still did not have the Bible in Malay at the time of the publication of this little book. Believing in Moses' authorship, Ruyl perhaps decided that the best way to reference this passage is by using number 5 to show that the text is actually taken from the fifth book of the Old Testament that was believed to have written by Moses. It is also interesting to see the broader use of *saboer* for a biblical book other than the Psalms. This is an indication that at the early stage of the presence of Reformed Protestantism, the ministers who came to the East Indies were not very concerned with regard to providing an exact, detailed way of referencing the Bible or biblical books. They seemed to be more concerned with providing basic teachings or doctrines and practices of the church than to teach the people details about the Bible. Therefore, as expressed in the *Sovrat ABC*, reference to Deuteronomy was loosely given as "the Psalm of Moses number 5, chapter 8."

---

21. Ruyl, *Sovrat ABC*, A7 verso.

The Place of Catechism in the Transplantation of Calvinism in the East Indies

The prayer after meals in the *Sovrat ABC* reflects the teaching of the Dutch Reformed church that people must be thankful to God for his blessings, especially in the form of food. The Deuteronomy passage shows that the Israelites should be thankful to God who brought them into the Promised Land, a land of milk and honey. For the children in the East Indies who read the *Sovrat ABC*, this passage reminded them to do the same. The insertion of this passage in the book indicates that reading the Deuteronomy passage was also customary in the Netherlands. As the school teachers and comforters of the sick led the children and the people in the prayers, this text became normative in shaping their minds to be thankful for all the blessings that God had given them. The prayer after meals in the *Sovrat ABC* is followed by a statement that the people should not fix their eyes on earthly wealth, but only look at Jesus Christ, who is in heaven, to be their great intercessor and mediator.

In late 1611 Reverend Jan Maertsz from Campen wrote a letter to the consistory in Amsterdam, reporting that there were two ships sailing from the Netherlands to the Indies. One of the ships, the Hollandia, which came out of Amsterdam, carried with it the *boeckxken van Aldegonde* that had been translated into Malay by Albert Corneliszoon Ruyl.[22] In this letter Maertsz explained that the book would be useful for the young children in Ambon to learn. This letter provides us a good look at how the copies of the catechetical material got transported from Amsterdam to the right destination.

In 1682, a second edition of the *Sovrat ABC* was published. It carries similar traits as the first edition, but also some clearly seen differences that could be perceived as improvements as well as further developments in the establishment of the Dutch Reformed church and a much stronger presence of the VOC in the East Indies. The first marked difference is evident in the title page. The new title of this small work is shortened and simplified to *Sourat A, B, C, Jang bergouna banja capada anac bouda*.[23] First of all, the spelling of the word *sourat* is noticeable. Instead of using "v" for the /u/ sound, the new title uses the letter "u." In English the new title simply means "ABC Letter, Which is Useful for Young Children." In the second edition there is no longer a statement that the book is intended to teach young children the beliefs of Christianity as taught to other Christians in other parts of the world.

22. SAA 379, Classis Amsterdam 19, no folio number.
23. Ruyl, *Sourat A, B, C*.

The Way to Heaven

The title page of the first edition of the *Sovrat ABC* has a woodcut picture of a classroom with young children sitting down on benches, a person that looks like a teacher sitting on a high chair in front of the group of children, and a young man standing in front of the teacher with an open book in his hands, giving the impression that this young man—a student—is reading from the open book to the teacher, with the rest of the students in class listening. This woodcut picture gives the readers a good visual aid of a teaching and learning scene in a seventeenth-century classroom. The woodcut picture on the title page of the second edition of the *Sourat ABC* shows a picture of a VOC ship. This woodcut picture is a clear demonstration that by 1682 the VOC had gained significant strength in the East Indies, and thus this title page sent a strong message that education and instruction for the young people in the archipelago must be done under the care of the VOC. In addition, the title page also explicitly states that this book was published "by the order of the directors of the chartered VOC."[24]

The first part of the second edition of the *Sourat ABC* is quite similar to the first edition, except that the fonts used to list the alphabet are larger than in the first. In the second edition, the title of the Ten Commandments is written in both Malay and Dutch.[25] The second edition does not mention that the Ten Commandments are taken from Exodus 20. There is significant difference in the translation of the Lord's Prayer in the second edition of the *Sourat ABC* compared to the first edition. In the second edition, the prayer is entitled *Bappa kita*, which literally means "Our Father." The Dutch title of the prayer also uses the first-person plural possessive case, *Onze Vader*.[26] The second edition demonstrated a development in the establishment of Reformed Protestantism in the East Indies. As the ministers did more work in the archipelago, they were able to provide a stronger foundation for the Protestant faith to grow, and the result was an expression of Protestantism that is more in line with the kind of Protestantism in Europe. Therefore, instead of privatizing the prayer into the first-person singular pronoun *hamba*, as was the case with the first edition, the second edition uses the common way of calling the prayer "Our Father." It is worth noting here that the pronoun used for the prayer here is *kita*. In Malay, the first-person plural pronoun for "we" and the possessive form "our" can take two

24. "Door ordre van de E. E. Heeren Bewinthebberen der Geoctroyeerde Oost-Indische Compagnie"; see title page of Ruyl, *Sourat A, B, C*, 1682.
25. Ruyl, *Sourat A, B, C*, A2 recto.
26. Ruyl, *Sourat A, B, C*, A5 recto.

The Place of Catechism in the Transplantation of Calvinism in the East Indies

forms. The word *kita* is an inclusive pronoun and is used when the speaker includes the interlocutor in the conversation. The word *kami* is an exclusive pronoun and used when the speaker does not include the interlocutor in the dialogue. In the later development of the Malay language which would then become the Indonesian language, the term *kami* or *Bapa kami* is more commonly used for the translation of the Lord's Prayer. Apparently, in the seventeenth century there was still no sharp distinction between *kami* and *kita* and therefore the second edition of the *Sourat ABC* uses *kita* instead of *kami* or *cammi*. The second edition of the *Sourat ABC* does not have the form for baptism. Also noticeable is the absence of instruction on how Christians should settle disputes among themselves as taught by Christ in Matthew 18. The form for the celebration of the Lord's Supper is titled only in Dutch, without its Malay translation, *Van het H. Hooghwaerdighe Nachtmael*.[27] Also, in this second edition there is a clear statement showing that the institution of the Lord's Supper is taken from 1 Corinthians 11:23–26.

Texts for morning prayer, evening prayer, and prayers for before and after meals are found in the second edition. Like in the first edition, the morning prayer includes the Lord's Prayer at the end.[28] Interestingly, in the text of the morning prayer, the Lord's Prayer is now called *Bappa cami*. As I already discussed earlier, in the second half of the seventeenth century there was still no consensus or consistence of when the word *kami* or *cami* and *kita* should be used, resulting in the variant uses of *Bappa cami* and *Bappa kita* for the Lord's Prayer.

The prayer before meals in the second edition of the *Sourat ABC* explicitly mentions the biblical text of Psalm 145:15–16 at the beginning. These two verses are printed with a slightly smaller font size and spacing before the text of the prayer itself to give clear indication that the biblical quote, though still a part of the prayer, is also a different kind of text.[29] In the second edition of the *Sourat ABC* there is no inclusion of the passage from Luke 21 that reminds people to avoid drunkenness.

The prayer after meals in the second edition has "Deut. 8 verss 10. 11" to show the biblical reference of the text. Unlike the first edition of the *Sovrat ABC*, which is not clear about the name of the book of Deuteronomy but calls it the "Psalm of Moses number 5," the second edition has shown further development in referencing biblical passages. Like the text for the

27. Ruyl, *Sourat A, B, C*, A5 verso.
28. Ruyl, *Sourat A, B, C*, A6 recto.
29. Ruyl, *Sourat A, B, C*, A7 recto.

prayer before meals, the biblical quote for this prayer is also printed separately from the text of the prayer, with a slightly smaller size of font and spacing. The inclusion of this biblical passage further indicates that by the second half of the seventeenth century Reformed people in the East Indies already had more familiarity with the Bible in Malay, so that the inclusion of the biblical text was considered useful and helpful to the readers in understanding that the prayer is actually based on that biblical passage.

The second edition of the *Sourat ABC* ends with the text of Psalm 100 in Malay, set to music. The psalm is written in metrical form, with each verse written in four lines, and each line has eight syllables. There are four verses in this versification of the psalm. The presence of the text and music of Psalm 100 in this edition is a further demonstration that by the time of its publication there was further development in the ecclesial practices of the Dutch Reformed churches in the East Indies. This further development is reflected in the tradition of psalm singing in Malay among the indigenous people of the East Indies. The versification of the psalm into metrical form is a clear reflection of the influence of the Genevan church's tradition of singing the psalm at the time of the Reformation. The tune that is used is the Genevan tune for Psalm 100 composed by Louis Burgeois in 1551.[30]

The 1682 edition of *Sourat ABC* ends with the list of cardinal numbers from one to thirty, then every ten, hundred, thousand, ten thousand and one hundred thousand. The numbers are written as Arabic numerals on the left column and in the Malay written form on the right column.[31]

De Spieghel vande Maleysche Tale

In 1612, a year after he published the *Sovrat ABC*, Albert Ruyl published the second catechetical material for young children in the East Indies. The title page of this work does not bear his name, but the dedicatory epistle to the directors of the VOC is signed by Ruyl.[32] In the dedicatory epistle Ruyl wrote that his intention in publishing this work was to spread the Christian faith in the East Indies, particularly to the young people.[33] Ruyl also wrote a letter to the readers, printed in both Dutch and Malay,[34] indicating that he

30. Ruyl, *Sourat A, B, C*, A8 recto.
31. Ruyl, *Sourat A, B, C*, A8 verso.
32. Ruyl, *Spieghel vande Maleysche Tale*, A2 recto–A3 recto.
33. Ruyl, *Spieghel*, A2 recto.
34. Ruyl, *Spieghel*, A3 verso–A4 recto.

The Place of Catechism in the Transplantation of Calvinism in the East Indies

printed this work with the intention that people who use this book could become righteous. In this letter he explained that those who did not understand who Christ is would also misunderstand Christianity. Therefore, he called the readers of this work to learn and to know the Christian religion, so that their hearts could be enlightened.[35]

The book includes both the original Dutch text and the Malay translation of the text. The texts are printed in columns where the left column has the Dutch text and the left column as the Malay translation. The first part of this book includes dialogues or play-like scripts interspersed with texts for prayers intended to help little children to learn the Christian faith and daily conduct as Christians. The first chapter is on what the chidren should do when they wake up in the morning. This lesson is constructed in the form of dialogues between characters named Abraham, Jacob, Solomon and David.[36] This dialogue is then followed by the text of morning prayer.[37] The text of this prayer is exactly the same as that of the morning prayer printed in the 1611 edition of the *Sovrat ABC*. The morning prayer ends with the Lord's Prayer. The entire text of the Lord's Prayer is included in this prayer, and it is also an identical text to the one printed in the 1611 edition of the *Sovrat ABC*.[38]

The second chapter of this book starts with another dialogue to teach the children some basic practices of Christianity, as well the proper manner of dealing with each other. The chapter starts with a dialogue between a teacher and three children, Zachariah, Joseph and Adam. The imagined setting of this dialogue is that the children are walking together to the central market and they meet their teacher on the way.[39] In the dialogue one finds that customs and vocabulary that are rooted in the Islamic culture and Arabic language are freely used. The most noted occurrence of this is the employment of the Arabic phrase *Salam-alaikum*, which the first character in the dialogue, Zachariah, says to his friend Joseph. This phrase is the standard greeting that Muslims say to each whenever they meet. It means "Peace be unto you." Following the standard politeness and hospitality among the

35. Ruyl, *Spieghel*, A4 recto.

36. Ruyl, *Spieghel*, A1 recto. The collation starts with A1 again, after A1–A4 of the preliminary material that includes the title page, the dedicatory epistle and the letter to the readers printed in Dutch and Malay.

37. Ruyl, *Spieghel*, A2 recto.

38. Ruyl, *Spieghel*, A1 verso, compare with Ruyl, *Sovrat ABC*, A4 verso.

39. In Malay, the names of the characters are Sacharia, Iusuf and Adam. See Ruyl, *Spieghel*, A2 verso.

Muslim community, the second character in the dialogue, Joseph, replies with the Arabic phrase *Alaikum salam*, which means "And peace unto you as well." Then, when Zechariah asks Joseph how he is doing, Joseph replies that he is just fine, and then ends his reply with another Arabic phrase, *Allaham dul Allah*, which means "I thank Allah." This little exchange in the dialogue shows us that at the beginning of the Dutch presence in the archipelago the Dutch ministers, most notably Ruyl, did not show any hesitance in using the customs and vocabulary of the Islamic community. The Dutch version of the dialogue uses the standard greetings in Dutch without the use of *Allah*. The first character greets the other with *Vreede sy met u*, and the second character replies by saying *Met u van ghelijcken*.[40]

The employment of Arabic phrases in the Malay translation of the dialogue is understandable because they were already widely used among the people in the archipelago even before the arrival of the Dutch. The employment of these phrases also indicates that at that time, among the inhabitants of the Indian archipelago, there was no hostility between the two religious groups. The fact that Ruyl freely employed these Arabic phrases also shows that the Dutch were indebted to the Islamic culture and community in their way of transplanting Christianity in the East Indies. Since language is a big part of cultural and religious assimilation and enculturation, the Dutch naturally used these words and phrases that were readily available to the indigenous people, even though these words and phrases were from a different religious group and were already loaded with meaning in that religion.

The dialogue in the second chapter ends with the children talking about moral issues such as stealing and lying. The dialogue was intended to put the teaching of the Ten Commandments into practice. The character of the teacher then appears in the scene and teaches the children that they should know the Lord's Prayer. At this point the text of the dialogue ends with the Lord's Prayer. What is significant to note in this section is that before mentioning the Lord's Prayer the character of the teacher tells the children that they should say the prayer in the name of *Allah*. The Malay dialogue uses the Arabic phrase *bismi Allah*.[41] Here we find another use of an Islamic custom. The Muslims, following the teaching of the Koran, always start any reading of a Koranic passage or prayer with the eaxact same Arabic phrase. It seems to us that Ruyl freely adopted this custom because he quite likely had seen this custom widely used among the indigenous

---

40. Ruyl, *Spieghel*, A2 verso.
41. Ruyl, *Spieghel*, A3 verso.

The Place of Catechism in the Transplantation of Calvinism in the East Indies

people. Considering that there is no harm in adopting the same custom, and that it would help new Christians in the archipelago to embrace the Christian teachings and beliefs, he openly accepted the custom.

The Malay translations of the Apostles' Creed and the Ten Commandments end the second chapter. Together with the Lord's Prayer included as an integral part of the dialogue, the creed and the Ten Commandments form the framework of the teaching of Christian faith for the readers of this book. It is clear for us that in the second chapter of this book Ruyl tries to show the children that they must know these three pillars of Christianity. They provide the most essential structure for them to understand Christianity.

The third chapter introduces the importance of prayers before and after each meal. The chapter starts with a dialogue that leads into prayer before breakfast. There are six characters in the dialogue: Moses, Samuel, Isaac, David, Abraham and the teacher.[42] The chapter opens with a dialogue between the children and the teacher as they are getting ready for breakfast. The dialogue is followed by the prayer before meal. The majority of the text of this prayer is similar to the prayer before meals included in the 1611 edition of *Sovrat ABC*, with some minor differences. The differences are mostly in the use of pronouns and some variations on sentence structure that do not alter the meaning of the sentences. In the *Sovrat ABC*, as it was his tendency, Ruyl chose to employ the first-person singular pronoun *hamba*, which has the connotation of a slave or servant before his master, to show the humility of the person offering the prayer.[43] In the *Spieghel* Ruyl tended to use the regular first-person singular *aku*, which literally means "I."[44]

The prayer before the meal in the *Spieghel* is followed by the biblical verse from Luke 21, just like that of the *Sovrat ABC*.[45] This reminder that people should not get drunk is perhaps used to remind the little children that when they grow up they should not subject themselves to the abuse of alcohol. Considering that the *Spieghel* was only published one year after the *Sovrat ABC*, we can see that Ruyl was sending the same message to the people in the East Indies, following the customs of the Reformed church in the Netherlands, that drunkenness is unacceptable. This biblical verse

---

42. Ruyl, *Spieghel*, B1 recto-verso.
43. [Ruyl, *Sovrat ABC*, A6 verso, and passim.
44. Ruyl, *Spieghel*, B1 verso and passim.
45. Ruyl, *Spieghel*, B1 verso, see also Ruyl, *Sovrat ABC*, A7 recto.

is then followed by another short dialogue between the children and the teacher. The dialogue ends with the teacher asking the children what they must remember regarding thankfulness. One of the children, Abraham, answers that the expression of thankfulness is written in "the Psalm of Moses, the fifth book, the eighth chapter."[46] The mention of this biblical passage, Deuteronomy 8, reminds us of the mention of the same passage in the prayer after meal in the *Sovrat ABC* of 1611.[47] However, this dialogue only cites the biblical address without giving the actual verse. In the context where the indigenous people still did not have the Bible in their vernacular, one wonders if this was an effective way of teaching the people. It seems useless to mention that a verse in the Bible talks about being thankful without showing what the biblical text really says. However, if one looks at both the *Sovrat ABC* and the *Spieghel* together, one could also argue that the two books should be used together as complements. If this was the case, then one could say that the two books together were meant to be used in tandem rather than separately.

The prayer for after meals ends the third chapter of the *Spieghel*. This prayer, in fact, starts with the quote from Deuteronomy 8, without stating that the text is a biblical one. Looking at the entire texts of the prayer before meals and after meals, one can see that this quote from Deuteronomy 8 directly follows the dialogue for before the meal in the previous section, where Abraham, the character in the dialogue, makes reference to the text. Thus, the mention of the fifth book of Moses in the dialogue before the meal is followed by the actual quote of Deuteronomy 8 in the prayer for after the meal, and together they form a unity. The problem in the way the texts are printed, however, is that the subtitle that shows that the following section is for the prayer for after meals causes one's mind to make a division between the two sections.

The fourth chapter of the *Spieghel* introduces the children to reading, writing and counting.[48] This chapter starts with a short dialogue among the children about the significance of reading and writing, followed by a list of the alphabet in two different fonts. After the list there is another dialogue, intended to encourage the children to learn how to write well. The dialogue is then followed by list of cardinal numbers, from one to twenty, then for each ten, hundred, thousand, ten thousand, one hundred thousand and one

---

46. Ruyl, *Spieghel*, B2 recto.
47. Ruyl, *Svrat ABC*, A7 verso.
48. Ruyl, *Spieghel*, B3 recto–C1 recto.

The Place of Catechism in the Transplantation of Calvinism in the East Indies

million, all in Arabic numerals, and spelled out in Dutch and Malay. This section is similar to the section at the end of the 1682 *Sourat ABC*, where Ruyl listed cardinal numbers written in Arabic numerals and spelled out in Malay. This section also teaches the children that there are 365 days in a year, 52 weeks in a year, and seven days in a week, together with the names of the months in each year in the Islamic calendar.[49] This section shows that in the earlier decades of the presence of the Dutch in the East Indies, the ministers were willing to accept what the Islamic culture had given the people. Ruyl did not see the need to force the people to use the Western names for the months. Instead, he openly accepted what the people already knew. What was important for them, as expressed in Ruyl's intention to publish this work, was to equip young children with the ability to read and write, while also to teach them some basic foundations of Reformed Protestantism. Since the names of months in Arabic did not hinder them from teaching the young children the basic teachings of Christian faith, they were willing to accept them as they were. In reality, in their daily lives the children had to use the Arabic names of the months.

The fifth chapter in this book is the longest one, containing the Malay translation of the children's catechism of Philip van Marnix.[50] The catechism is printed in two columns, with the left column written in Dutch and the right column in Malay translation. The entire catechism has 212 questions. The same catechism was also translated into Portuguese and published as a separate publication for the Portuguese-speaking community in the East Indies. Abraham Rogerio, a preacher in Batavia, translated that version of the catechism.[51] This Portuguese translation was also printed under the order of the directors of the VOC. The title page of the Portuguese version has a similar woodcut as the 1682 edition of the *Sourat ABC*, with the picture of a VOC ship proudly sailing across the ocean. When one sees the catechism of van Marnix in the Malay and Portuguese translations, one can get a clear sense that the VOC had the intention of providing catechetical instruction to both the Malay- and Portuguese-speaking children in the archipelago. The Malay edition of van Marnix's catechism is followed by another short dialogue between the children and the teacher, focusing on the significance for young children to be obedient to their parents and to

49. Ruyl, *Spieghel*, B4 verso.
50. Ruyl, *Spieghel*, C1 verso–F1 recto.
51. Rogerio, *Compendioso Exame dos Principaes Puntos de Religiaõ Christaõ Composto*.

31

obey the teaching of Jesus. As the church order of Batavia of 1643 indicates, in the regions where Portuguese was still heavily used, the school teachers must catechize people using the Portuguese catechism. The *Compendio* therefore functioned as one of the main texts that the school teachers had to use in those regions.

The last two chapters of the *Spieghel* have more dialogues that are constructed as short skits to help the children learn several basic teachings of Christian faith as well as good manners as Christians.[52] There is an emphasis on obedience to parents and teachers in these two chapters. It seems that the Dutch ministers wanted to make sure that the children learned the proper way of addressing their superiors. While respect for elders is a part of the Ten Commandments, which all Christians must follow, the emphasis here tends to be that the children obey the Dutch as their new rulers. In the time when the VOC was trying to establish its power over the land, one wonders that any commands to obey one's superiors would finally have the ultimate goal that obedience to their authority is a reflection of obedience to God. Therefore, since they are still very young, the children have been told that part of their religious duty is also to obey the Dutch authority, because God has placed the Dutch as the power over them. The seventh chapter ends with evening prayer[53] and the Lord's Prayer, with the same text as printed earlier in the book.[54]

The *Spieghel* includes a simple Dutch-Malay dictionary that is printed following the seven chapters of instructional material for young children. The dictionary is printed in two columns, with the left column containing Dutch words arranged in alphabetical order and the right column with the Malay synonym of each word. In the edition that I am using for this research, the collation starts with A1 again, giving the impression that the dictionary had been printed independently from the original printing of the *Spieghel*.[55] In this particular copy the two works were simply bound together. The dictionary section is entitled *Vocabularium van de Duytsche ende Maleysche tale nae de ordre van't alphabet*.[56] At the end of the dictionary, after the last word under "Z" is listed, the dictionary has a shorter list

---

52. Ruyl, *Spieghel*, F2 recto–H2 recto.
53. Ruyl, *Spieghel*, G4 verso.
54. Ruyl, *Spieghel*, H1 recto–H2 recto.
55. In this particular edition the dictionary runs from A1 recto to K4 recto.
56. Ruyl, *Spieghel*, A1 recto, back part.

The Place of Catechism in the Transplantation of Calvinism in the East Indies

of words pertaining to human being in general, including terms body parts as well as for familial relationships, in Dutch and translated into Malay.[57]

In 1682, another version of the Malay translation of van Marnix's catechism was published by Paulus Matthysz in Amsterdam.[58] There is no mention of the full name of the translator in this printed work. The letter to the readers is signed by a person with the initials S. D. In the letter S. D. acknowledges that the same catechism had been translated into Malay by Ruyl. In addition, S. D. also indicates that this small book was intended for the people in Ambon, Banda and the rest of the Moluccas islands.[59] A close comparison with the earlier edition of the catechism translated by Ruyl in 1612 reveals that the newer translation shows further development of the use of Malay in the Christian circles in the East Indies. The questions in this newer edition are not numbered. Unlike Ruyl's translation, which uses the Arabic term *Allah* for God, this 1682 edition uses the Portuguese term, *Deos*. The use of pronouns between the two editions also shows further development in the use of Malay. The 1612 edition uses *angkou* for the second-person singular pronoun[60] whereas the 1682 edition uses *camou*.[61] This shift is significant. As it became more obvious in the later development of the Malay language into Indonesian, the use of *camou*, which was later spelled as *kamu*, turned to be the more acceptable choice of word for the second-person singular pronoun.

A comparison between the two editions also shows that as time progressed, spelling became more standardized and the later development in spelling was then adopted in the modern-day spelling of Indonesian words. There are some examples to be cited here. The first noticeable example is the spelling of the Malay word for "human being." In the earlier edition the word is spelled *manusea* but in the later edition it is spelled *manusia*, and the latter is the one adopted in modern Indonesian.[62] Another significant distinction is the use of the word *eklesia*[63] for church in Ruyl's translation

---

57. Ruyl, *Spieghel*, K3 recto–K4 recto.

58. *Adjaran dalam Jang Manna Jadi Caberadjar Capalla Capallanja derri Agamma Christaon.*

59. *Adjaran*, A1 verso.

60. Ruyl, *Spieghel*, C2 recto, and passim.

61. *Adjaran*, A2 recto and passim.

62. Ruyl, *Spieghel*, C2 recto and passim; and *Adjaran*, A2 recto and passim.

63. Ruyl, *Spieghel*, C3 recto

and the word *igresia*[64] in the 1682 edition of the catechism. The move from the adoption of the Greek word *ekklesia* for "church" in the earlier edition to the Portuguese loan-word signifies the move to use a more familiar term. Even though Greek was as foreign as Portuguese for the people, at least they were more familiar with Portuguese than they were with Greek, even though Greek is the original language of the New Testament. Perhaps Ruyl decided to use *eklesia* in his translation of the catechism because there was no term for "church" in Malay then. The later translator's decision to use the Portuguese word *igresia*, however, proved to be a more preferred approach. It turns out that the term stayed in the vocabulary of the East Indies, and modern-day Indonesian word for "church" is *gereja*, which is the adaptation and transliteration of the seventeenth-century Portuguese word *igresia*.

The concepts of the cross and crucifixion were foreign to the indigenous people of the East Indies. The Dutch ministers who went to the archipelago in the earliest period of the VOC must have realized that the people did not know the deep, religious, uniquely Christian meaning of the cross. In the 1612 edition of the van Marnix catechism included in the *Spieghel*, Ruyl translated the "cross" as *kakrus*.[65] This word might have been a combination of the Malay preposition *ke*, which means "on" or "to" or "onto," and *krus*, the adaptation of the word *kruis* or *cruz* for "cross." The combination of the preposition and the noun might likely be caused by the context in which the word is used. The word appears for the first time in answer 56 of the catechism. In the context of the catechism, question and answer 55 explain how Christ carried the curse of sin on himself.[66] Then question 56 asks "where" (where did Christ carry the curse of sin on himself), and the answer is *kakrus*, "on or to the cross." The rest of the 1612 edition of the catechism uses *kakrus* for the cross. The 1682 edition shows more refined choice of word. It uses *cayou-cruz*,[67] literally meaning "[the] wooden cross." It is easy for the readers to identify that *cruz* must have been the European loan-word for "cross." The word *cayou* in Malay means "wood" or "wooden." The introduction of the word *cayou* into the concept of the cross turned out to be a favorable option because it made the meaning of Jesus' cross more real for the people. It is true that the Bible says Jesus was hung on a tree. The addition of the word *cayou* enabled the people to

64. *Adjaran*, A3 recto.
65. Ruyl, *Spieghel*, C4 verso, D1 recto and passim.
66. Ruyl, *Spieghel*, C4 verso.
67. *Adjaran*, A6 recto and passim.

The Place of Catechism in the Transplantation of Calvinism in the East Indies

picture what the cross is. The word *cayou* stayed in the vocabulary of the church in the East Indies and into modern-day Indonesia.

The translations of the catechism took some Arabic loan-words to translate certain theological concepts. Both editions use the Arabic *califfa* for "priest," as evidenced in the translation of questions and answers 118 and 119, in which the catechism focuses on Christ as the anointed priest for his people.[68] Similarly, the translators also adopted the Arabic words *nabi* for "prophet"[69] and *narca* or *neraca* for "hell."[70] These Arabic loan-words later became integral parts of the vocabulary of the churche in the East Indies, beyond the bounds of Reformed Protestantism.

The Malay Translation of the Heidelberg Catechism, 1623

Sebastian Danckaerts translated and published the Heidelberg Catechism in Malay in 1623. In his dedicatory epistle to the directors of the VOC and to the governors of the provinces of the Netherlands, he stated that as he ministered in Ambon (or Amboina) he saw that a translation of the catechism was highly needed. He emphasized that the people needed a catechism book that was used by the Reformed church in their own language.[71] Danckaerts acknowledged that there were different languages used in the region, but Malay was the language that people in that particular quarter—Ambon—used and understood.

As the title page of the translation of the catechism indicates—*Catechismus attau Adjaran derri agamma Christaon. Bersalin derri bahassa Hollanda dalam Bahassa Maleya*—Danckaerts emphasized the fact that the catechism was intended as the teaching of the Christian religion. The Malay word *adjaran* means "teaching." This emphasis on the teaching of the Christian religion showed that the translation of the catechism was meant to be the first and most important step in providing the new Christians with what they should know regarding their religion, or more particularly, their faith. Nowhere in this catechism is the name "Heidelberg" mentioned. This is an indication that Danckaerts and other Dutch ministers working in the East Indies did not want to burden the new Christians in the East Indies with the details about the name and origin of the catechism. The people did

68. Ruyl, *Spieghel*, D4 recto; and *Adjaran*, A9 recto.
69. Ruyl, *Spieghel*, D4 verso and passim; and *Adjaran*, A10 verso.
70. Ruyl, *Spieghel*, E2 verso; and *Adjaran*, A11 verso.
71. Danckaerts, *Catechismus attau Adjaran derri agamma Christaon*, *3 recto.

not need to know where the catechism originated. What they needed to know was the content of the teaching of their new religion.

The Malay translation of the Heidelberg Catechism follows the format of the catechism that the Reformed churches in Europe had. After the first two questions and answers, which focus on the only comfort that believers have in life and in death,[72] the rest of the catechism is divided into three parts, respectively on the topics of sin, salvation and service. Danckaerts also followed the standard practice of the Reformed churches in Europe in grouping the 129 questions and answers into 52 Lord's Days. In this translation he used the Malay word *Ahad*, which means "Sunday."[73] The use of the term *Ahad* for Sunday is consistent with Ruyl's use of the same term in his explanation of the days of the week that he intended for young children in his *Spieghel*.[74]

Danckaerts provided a somewhat lengthy title for the first part of the catechism on sin and misery. In the Malay translation of the catechism Danckaerts used the title *Derri manusia pounja coutoc daen sixa, nang Tuan Deos talla sudah bri pada manusia taghal dosa*.[75] In English, this title means: "From the curse and suffering of human beings that the Lord God has given to human beings because of sin." This title is obviously longer than the common title used in the Dutch version of the catechism, *Van des menschen elende*. As the title indicates, Danckaerts seemed to want to emphasize the fact that human suffering is caused by sin, and that sin carries with it a curse. By providing this longer translation of the title, Danckaerts demonstrated that he wanted the people to know that the cause of human suffering is sin. However, it is also interesting to see that he attributed the cause of the curse—and the suffering—as God himself. There seems to be a direct causation that Danckaerts was willing to make, namely that God is the active cause of suffering. Danckaerts expanded his thought in the translation of the third question of the catechism. Danckaerts' edition posts the the third question as: "How do you know about your curse and suffering which the Lord God has given to human beings because of sin?" The expansion of the question seems to be Danckaerts' effort to show that God as the sovereign Lord of the universe dislikes sin, and the suffering or misery that humans now have is because of their sin. The sovereignty of God,

72. Danckaerts, *Catechismus*, A1 recto–verso.
73. Danckaerts, *Catechismus*, passim.
74. Ruyl, *Spieghel*, B4 recto.
75. Danckaerts, *Catechismus*, A2 recto.

The Place of Catechism in the Transplantation of Calvinism in the East Indies

Danckaerts seems to have been saying, includes the fact that sin does not escape from God's knowledge, and even though God is not the cause of sin, the punishment or the curse of sinmcomes from God directly.

The second part of the catechism is entitled *Bagaimanna manusia menjadi lepas attau toubous derri dosa, lagi dosa pounja houcoum*,[76] meaning: "How human beings can be free or redeemed from sin, [and] more importantly, from the punishment of sin?" This title, like the title of the first part of the catechism, is an expansion of the commonly accepted versions of the catechism in Europe. Most editions of the catechism only use the title "Deliverance" for the second part. The Dutch version of the catechism uses a somewhat longer title: *Van des menschen verlossing*. In the Malay translation of the catechism Danckaerts showed indication that he wanted to be descriptive in translating the catechism. He wanted to show that the second section is about the redemption of human beings from the punishment of sin, to emphasize the great redemptive work of Christ. It seems to us that for Danckaerts the title of each section ought to convey as much meaning as possible so that the new Christians in the archipelago would be able to understand the catechism well. With such clear title for each section, there is no doubt that the readers of this catechism would find it easier to understand the teaching of each section of the catechism.

In the second section of the catechism, in translating "God" and the "Trinity" in the questions and answers dealing with the explanation of the Apostles' Creed, Danckaerts was not hesitant to use Portuguese words that were already introduced to the people of the East Indies by the Jesuit missionaries. In his translation of the Heidelberg Catechism he used the term *Deos Bapa* to translate "God the Father," *Deos Anak* for "God the Son" and *Spirito Santo* for the Holy Spirit.[77] *Deos* is the Portuguese word for God, and the word *bapa* is the Malay word for "father" and *anak* is the Malay word for "son" or "child." In the dictionary, in the entry for the Dutch word *Godt*, he explained that Malay did not have its own word for God. The Muslims, he wrote, use the Arabic word *Allah*. Since the people in Ambon and other islands in the Moluccas were already familiar with the Portuguese word *Deos*, he saw it right to use the word *Deos* for God.[78]

---

76. Danckaerts, *Catechismus*, A3 verso.
77. Danckaerts, *Catechismus*, passim.
78. Wiltens and Danckaerts, *Vocabularium*, 25.

Danckaerts gave the third part of the Heidelberg Catechism the title *Bagaimana cami memalasken Tuan Deos pounja fermang daen cassie*,[79] meaning: "How we can repay the words and the love of [our] Lord God." The title is Danckaerts' way of explaining what gratitude means. It shows us that for him, gratitude means to repay or to return what God has done for his people. He also focused on two particular items that God has done for his people, namely his words and his love. Danckaerts' employment of God's words as the great gift that God has given to his people is noteworthy. It seems to us that Danckaerts wanted to tell the people that the gift of salvation is almost identical with God's words. Perhaps he meant that God's word is the equivalent of the good news of the gospel. At the same time, he also showed that God's great gift is his love, out of which redemption—the main topic of the second part of the catechism—flows. Therefore, in the third part of the catechism, he wanted the readers to understand that they must repay God for these great gifts that God has given.

Danckaerts included prayers for before and after preaching in his Malay translation of the Heidelberg Catechism. This inclusion seemed to be his effort to continue the practice of the Reformed church in the Netherlands. Even though he did not include other standardized prayers that the Reformed church in the Netherlands had, the inclusion of these two prayers is an indication that Danckaerts appreciated the practice of his church in the homeland, and that he wanted to transplant that practice in the East Indies. By having the prayers in the catechism book he could make sure that other ministers in the East Indies would use the prayers, and this would in turn ensure the orthodoxy and orthopraxy of the new Reformed churches in the East Indies. This inclusion also shows similarity between Danckaerts' translation of the Heidelberg Catechism and Ruyl's *Sovrat ABC* of 1611.

De Wegh na den Hemel

In September of 1657 Josias Spiljardus completed his Malay translation of a small catechism book which he entitled *Djalang ca Surga*, meaning "The Way to Heaven." Spiljardus came to Batavia in 1656 and was then sent to minister in Banda and on the island of Pulaoe-Aij. From there he moved to Ambon in 1658. He returned to the Netherlands in 1666.[80] In the manuscript of the translation, Spiljardus wrote to the readers that this

---

79. Danckaerts, *Catechismus*, C5 recto.
80. Bruijn, *Biographisch Woordenboek*, 409.

The Place of Catechism in the Transplantation of Calvinism in the East Indies

small catechism book, which he called *Kitab Taniahan kitsjil*, "The Small Question Book," is a guide for going to heaven.[81] In his letter he wanted the readers to learn from the catechism book because it contained the foundation of the teachings of the Christian religion. He also explained that in this translation he included citations from the Scriptures so that the readers could see the source of the teaching. He intended that the direct quotations or citations from Scripture be printed using different a font so that it would be easy for the readers to distinguish between the teaching of the catechism and the quotes from the Bible.[82]

The small catechism is the translation of the Zeeland Catechism that was affirmed at the synod of Zeeland in the city of Goes in 1620.[83] The original catechism was written by Willem Teellinck, under the title *Den Wegh ter Saligheyd*.[84] Teellinck (1579–1629) was a minister of Middelburg starting in 1612. He was one of the most prominent leaders of Pietism the Netherlands.[85] Like the original catcheism, *De Wegh na den Hemel* also has forty-six questions and answers.

The title of the Malay translation of this catechism book reflects Spiljardus' understanding of the context of religious life in the East Indies. While Teellinck called the small catechism *Den Wegh ter Saligheyd*, "The Way to Salvation," Spiljardus chose the title *De wegh na den Hemel*, "The Way to Heaven," for the new Christians in the Indies. Even though the two titles reflect the same concept, that the catechism book teach the people how to be saved in Christ, Spiljardus' Malay translation spoke more directly to the indigenous people. In light of polemics with Islam, which also emphasized how people could go to heaven, Spiljardus directly took the step of showing that the content of his small catechism book is the true answer for the people about how they can go to heaven. The catechism provides the answer that following the Reformed faith would assure that the people would enter heaven. The catechism was also meant to show polemics against Roman Catholicism. The Roman Catholics emphasized the significance of sacraments, especially baptism, to guarantee entrance into heaven. As evidenced from the content of the catechism, in the Calvinist

---

81. Spiljardus, *Djalang ca Surga*, fol. 48.

82. Spiljardus, *Djalang ca Surga*, fol. 49.

83. Spiljardus, *Djalang ca Surga*, fol. 47. For more description on the synod of Zeeland in 1620, see Hof, "De Nadere Reformatie in Zeeland."

84. Uil, "De Nadere Reformatie en het onderwijs."

85. Engelberts, *Willem Teellinck*, 26.

faith sacraments are not the way to heaven. Knowing the teachings of the Bible would bring people to the knowledge of the one true God, and thus would show people the way into heaven.

The first question of the catechism indicates this emphasis: *Appa itou nang mou souca daen minta terlebe?*, meaning "What is your greatest desire?" or "What do you want the most?" The answer is *Agar beta dapat massoc dalam Surga*, or "That I can enter heaven."[86] This first question and answer is a clear reflection of the Reformed church's effort to show the new believers in the East Indies that eternal salvation should be their greatest desire. And the teaching of the Reformed church as the way to heaven is fully spelled out in the catechism. Thus, as against Islamic people, who also desire to go to heaven but do not have a clear answer as to how they can get there, the Reformed faith provides a clear, definite answer. And against the Roman Catholics, who taught salvation by way of doing the sacraments, the entire catechism spells out that salvation is through Jesus Christ who is the center of God's redemptive work.

The next three questions of the *Wegh na den Hemel* set the stage for further teaching of how people can get to heaven. The second question asks, "Where do you find written explanation about the way to heaven?" The answer is: "In the Word of God."[87] Questions and answers 3 and 4 follow the pattern given in the Heidelberg Catechism. Question 3 asks, "What does the Word of God teach you, in order that you can go to heaven? Answer: "Three things." Question 4: "What are they?" Answer: "My suffering, my redemption and my gratitude."[88] From there the catechism moves on, following the Heidelberg Catechism, to the questions and answers on sin, salvation and service. The rest of the catechism is basically a shorter and simplified version of the Heidelberg Catechism. Spiljardus seemed to prefer the idea of sin as suffering, and therefore in the first part of the catechism, where it discusses the misery of sinful human beings, he deliberately chose the Malay word *sixa*, meaning "torture" or "suffering."

As he wrote in the preface of this translation, Spiljardus took the time to cite biblical passages to support the answer to each question. While by the time Spiljardus translated the catechism the whole Bible was not yet translated into Malay, his effort to provide biblical passages to support the catechism could function as a supplement for the Bible to help the people

---

86. Spiljardus, *Djalang ca Surga*, fol. 49.
87. Spiljardus, *Djalang ca Surga*, fol. 51.
88. Spiljardus, *Djalang ca Surga*, fol. 52.

understand. By providing a full quotation of each biblical verse he cited, Spiljardus was able to show the people that the teaching of the Reformed church that he presented was strongly rooted in the word of God.

Like Danckaerts in his translation of the Heidelberg Catechism, Spiljardus used the Portuguese term *Deos* for God.[89] This indicates that toward the middle of the seventeenth century the Dutch ministers were still indebted to the Portuguese language to help transplant theological concepts in the minds of the new Christians in the East Indies. The indebtedness to the Portuguese language is also reflected in the use of the term *igresia* for "church."[90] This choice has stayed in the vocabulary of Christians in the East Indies for centuries.

Spiljardus included the whole text of the Apostles' Creed in the answer to question 19 of the catechism, about what exactly Christians believe.[91] In translating the creed he consistently used the first-person singular pronoun *beta*, which is a clear indication that he had the Ambonese as his main audience. There is marked distinction between the Ambonese and the rest of the East Indian archipelago's use of the pronoun. The rest of the East Indies uses *saya* for "I," whereas the Ambonese use *beta*. Also noteworthy here is the fact that Spiljardus started each article of the creed with *Beta pitsjaja*, meaning "I believe," which shows that he wanted to be consistent in his translation to help the Ambonese Christians to memorize the creed. Having such a formulaic statement of belief, the people would find it easier to understand the basic teaching of the Christian faith. As a contrast, we find that Ruyl took a slightly different approach in translating the creed in his *Sovrat ABC*. Ruyl used the first-person singular pronoun *hamba* only on the first and eighth articles of the creed.[92] As discussed above, Ruyl's use of *hamba* showed that the person who is speaking to God, whether in prayer or in confession, shows humility, like a servant being humble in the presence of his or her master. In addition, Ruyl's choice of using *hamba* indicates that he had an audience that was larger than just the Ambonese Christians for his small catechetical material.

Spiljardus borrowed the Islamic concept of the last judgment when he translated the eleventh article of the creed. His translation shows the need for him to interpret what resurrection of the body means. In the catechism

89. Spiljardus, *Djalang ca Surga*, question and answer 21, and passim.
90. Spiljardus, *Djalang ca Surga*, question and answer 30, and passim.
91. Spiljardus, *Djalang ca Surga*, question and answer 19.
92. Ruyl, *Sovrat ABC*, A4 recto–verso.

he wrote, *Beta pitsjaja badang segalla manusia nang mati coumbali idop pada hari kiamat,*[93] meaning, "I believe [that] the bodies of all humans will live again on judgment day." The term that the Islamic people use for Judgment Day is *hari kiamat,* and the term has the connotation of a cataclysmic event and day of fear and terror when the end of time comes. Spiljardus' adoption of the term helped him explain to Christians in Ambon that the resurrection happens in the end time, but the choice of *hari kiamat* planted the idea in the minds of Christians in the archipelago that the end time, or the second coming of Christ, will be a terrifying time instead of a joyous, glorious time when the resurrected believers will be united with the risen Christ. This translation is different from that of Ruyl, who simply translated the "resurrection of the body" almost literally: *Daen bangkitan daging badan,*[94] or "And the resurrection of the flesh of the body."

In 1683 Franchois Caron, a long-time minister in Ambon who later in his life returned to the Netherlands to minister in Lexmonde, published an almost identical small catechism book, which he entitled *De Wegh na den Hemel.* The title page does not have a publication date, but Caron signed his dedicatory epistle on March 18, 1683.[95] The title page of this published work bears close similarity with Spiljardus' translation of *Djalang ca Surga.* In fact, the Dutch title that Caron used in this published work is exactly the translation of *Djalang ca surga,* namely, "The Way to Heaven." The title page says that this small question book, or the *vraegh-boecksken,* is intended for those who are just beginning as Christians, and that this catechism was based on the same that was affirmed by the synod of Zeeland in the city of Goes in 1620. It also states that the catechism book includes biblical quotations.[96] On the title page Caron stated that this small catechism is his own work, translated out of Low Dutch into Malay, for the education of Christians in the East Indian archipelago. The second page of the catechism book has a full quote from Proverbs 22:6 in Dutch and Malay. The same biblical verse is also used by Spiljardus in the manuscript of his *Djalang ca surga.*[97]

---

93. Spiljardus, *Djalang ca Surga,* fol. 62.

94. Ruyl, *Sovrat ABC,* A4 verso.

95. Caron, *De Wegh na den Hemel,* A2 verso.

96. Caron, *De Wegh na den Hemel,* title page, A1 recto. See also Spiljardus, *Djalang ca Surga,* fol. 47.

97. Caron, *De Wegh na den Hemel,* A1 verso. See also Spiljardus, *Djalang ca Surga,* fol. 47.

The Place of Catechism in the Transplantation of Calvinism in the East Indies

Caron did not mention his indebtedness to Spiljardus in his dedicatory epistle. He only mentioned that he was very thankful to the directors of the VOC that the small catechism was finally printed. He also stated that he saw the great need for the Ambonese Christians to have the catechism book printed in Malay, considering that the catechism of the synod of Zeeland was very important for Christians. He also showed that the use of biblical quotes in the catechism was necessary for the readers. He wrote that first of all this catechism book could be used in schools, together with the catechism of van Marnix and also the Heidelberg Catechism. But because the other two catechism materials did not have biblical quotations in them, this catechism book with its biblical citations became much more useful.[98]

It is puzzling why Caron did not mention Spiljardus' name as the source or first translator of this work, while it essentially is the same work. It could very well be that Caron only saw the manuscript of Spiljardus' catechism without knowing that Spiljardus was the first translator. The resemblance between the manuscript and the printed work is so close, however, giving the impression that Caron simply just put his name on the printed work after making some minor modifications.

Caron made some minor changes in the wording of the catechism of Spiljardus. His modifications showed his efforts to make the language of the catechism more easily understood by the Ambonese. He mostly rearranged the sentence structures to suit the catechism better for the readers. For instance, Spiljardus wrote the first question as: *Appa itou nang mou souca daen minta terlebe?*[99] In English, the meaning of this sentence is: "What is this, that you like and ask the most?" Caron, on the other hand, wrote a smoother Malay sentence: *Appala itou, jang mou terlebe souca daan minta?*[100], translated as "What do you mostly love and that you ask for?" Caron's use of the particle *la* in the word *apalla* made the sentence smoother for the Malay readers. Besides, his rearrangement of the word order made the meaning of the whole questions more understandable. In the answer to the first question Caron inserted a word that brought more urgency in the sentence. Unlike Spiljardus, who straightforwardly answered the question by saying *Agar beta masouc dalam surga* or "So that I can enter heaven," Caron wrote *Agar beta dapat massoc Surga* or "So that I can enter heaven."

---

98. Caron, *De Wegh na den Hemel*, A2 verso.
99. Spiljardus, *Djalang ca Surga*, 58.
100. Caron, *De Wegh na den Hemel*, 5.

The urgency of wanting to enter heaven is expressed through the use of the word *dapat*, which means "can" or "to be able to."

Caron took a softer approach in translating or explaining the first part of the catechism, on the misery of human beings because of sin. He wrote that the first thing humans must know is their shame. In the catechism Caron used the word *caibana*,[101] meaning "shamefulness." This is a somewhat different approach compared to Spiljardus, who preferred using the word for suffering or even torture, *sixa*, which humans undergo because of sin.[102] Caron thus entitled the first part of the catechism as *Deri Kaibana Manusia*,[103] meaning "On the Shame of Human Beings."

It is also noteworthy that by the time Caron served in the East Indies in the latter part of the seventeenth century, the term *Allah* was used to refer to God. This is to show that there was more familiarity with Islam, and that the Reformed ministers were no longer hesitated in using the term *Allah* to refer to God. As discussed above, Spiljardus consistently used the Portuguese word *Deos* for God. Caron was more comfortable in borrowing the Arabic term *Allah*.[104] Like Spiljardus, and unlike Danckarts in his translation of the Heidelberg Catechism, Caron already transitioned from the use of more Portuguese-influenced names for the Trinity to purely Malay and some Arabic-influenced names. Caron and Spiljardus used *Allah Bappa* for "God the Father," *Allah Anac* for "God the Son" and *Ruah Ulcadus* for the "Holy Spirit."[105] The term *Ruah Ulcadus* is borrowed from Arabic. *Ruah* is the Arabic word for "spirit" and "*ulcadus*" is the Arabic for "holy."

Caron translated the Apostles' Creed more freely and less formulaicly than Spiljardus. He only used the formula *Beta pitsjaja* or "I believe" for the first, eighth and ninth articles, the ones dealing with belief in God the Father Almighty, belief in the Holy Spirit and belief in the holy catholic church respectively.[106] His transition from the first to the second articles followed the custom that the creed was commonly recited in Europe by saying, "I believe in God the Father Almighty, creator of heaven and earth, and in Jesus Christ . . ." And unlike Spiljardus, who borrowed the concept of

---

101. Caron, *De wegh na den Hemel*, 6.
102. Spiljardus, *Djalang ca Surga*, question and answer 4.
103. Caron, *De Wegh na den Hemel*, 8.
104. Caron, *De Wegh na den Hemel*, questions 6, 7, 8, 21 and passim.
105. Caron, *De Wegh na den Hemel*, question and answer 21; Spiljardus, *Djalang ca Surga*, question and answer 21.
106. Caron, *De Wegh na den Hemel*, 17.

the end time from Islam in his translation of the eleventh article, Caron just translated the article as *jang bangonan deri dagin*, meaning "the resurrection of flesh."[107] By translating this article simply, Caron avoided complications from having to borrow the concept from the Islamic religion. Even though Spiljardus' attempt may sound more practical because he used the term *hari kiamat*, which was already used by the majority of the people in the East Indies given their familiarity with Islam, his use posed other complications. Caron, on the other hand, took a less complicated step, doing as what Ruyl did in his translation, simply stating that the eleventh article is about the resurrection of the body or the flesh.

Like the Heidelberg Catechism, *De Wegh na den Hemel* ends with the explanation of the Lord's Prayer. What deserves our attention, however, are questions and answers 45 and 46. Spiljardus wrote question 45 as: "What do you ask from God of all gods in worshipping in all this"? Here Spiljardus connected the prayer with worshipping God. The answer to this question is that people will glorify God and that they will receive blessing from God. Caron, on the other hand, phrased question 45 differently. His version of the question is: "What exactly do you ask from God [*Allah*] in all the requests?" Answer: "That I glorify God in all things, and that I receive salvation." While Spiljardus emphasized blessing for the people who pray the Lord's Prayer, Caron emphasized the granting of eternal salvation to the ones offering prayer to the true God. We see again Caron's emphasis on getting eternal salvation in this answer, so as to form bookends with the opening questions of the catechism. And to wrap everything together, question 46 asks: "Tell me, what in the end happens to you, if you follow all of these?" The question is rather ambiguous because it does not specify what it means by "all of these." But looking at the entire purpose of the catechism, we could say that it perhaps means everything that the catechism teaches. And this is confirmed by the answer: "I can be free from my curse and misery, and therefore I can go to heaven." Spiljardus and Caron showed agreement with each other in closing the catechism with answer 46. They showed that people will be freed from the misery of their sin and will enter heaven. And in their translations each minister was consistent with the choice of words they took all along. Spiljardus stated that by keeping all the teachings of the catechism people will be delivered from their *sixa*, or "torture" or "suffering," because of their sin.[108] Caron used the terms *cout-*

---

107. Caron, *De Wegh na den Hemel*, 17.
108. Spiljardus, *Djalang ca Surga*, answer 46.

ouc dan tsilacca,[109] "curse and misery," to show the effects of sin from which believers are delivered.

---

109. Caron, *De Wegh na den Hemel*, 32.

2

The Sermons of Wiltens and Danckaerts as Tools for the Early Establishment of Calvinism in the East Indies

Caspar Wiltens' Sermons

CASPAR WILTENS WAS THE first minister to arrive in the East Indies. He came to the archipelago in 1611, when he was only twenty-seven years old. Between 1612 and 1615 he ministered on the islands of Bacan and Banda. Later in 1615 he moved to Ambon, where he served until he returned to the Netherlands in 1621.[1] While he was ministering in the East Indies he preached several sermons. The collection of his sermons was eventually published in 1648. Justus Heurnius wrote the preface to the published sermons.[2] In his preface Heurnius praised Wiltens for the quality of his sermons and the fine Malay language that Wiltens used.[3] The collection is divided into fourteen titled sermons. However, within each titled sermon there are two sermons of the same topic that Wiltens apparently delivered over two consecutive Sundays. The second part of the sermon is given subtitle *Het andere deel*.[4] Therefore, even though the title of the printed work indicates that there are fourteen sermons,

1. End, *Ragi Carita*, 256.
2. Justus Heurnius, "Voor-reden aen de E. Bedinaers des Heyligen Euangelii, in Oost-India," in Wiltens, *Maleysche Predicatien*, *2 recto–verso.
3. Justus Heurnius, "Voor-reden aen de E. Bedinaers des Heyligen Euangelii, in Oost-India," in Wiltens, *Maleysche Predicatien*, *A verso.
4. Wiltens, *Maleysche Predicatien*, passim.

47

in reality there are twenty-eight sermons by Wiltens in the collection. The sermons were printed on double-column pages with each column containing approximately thirty-five lines. Each line has about six words. There are about 420 words per page, and each sermon is about six pages long, making the length of each sermon approximately 2520 words each. When read with a normal speed, the sermon would last for about thirty to forty-five minutes.

Wiltens arranged his sermons in such a way that they functioned as teaching tools for the new believers in the Reformed faith. His sermons were doctrinal in nature, without much exposition of biblical texts. Reading the printed sermons, one gets the impression of reading lectures on systematic theology wrapped in the rhetorical style of a sermon. The fourteen titles of the twenty-eight sermons published in the collection more or less followed the standard topics of scholastic methodology. He started with a general view of God and his works in creation, including the creation of angels. The first sermon functioned as an overarching introduction of what Reformed Protestant faith is about, especially on the topic of the relationship between God and creation. The second sermon brought its audience to look at God's general and special revelation, with the emphasis on the Scriptures as God's words. The third sermon covered the theme of the nature of God. He entitled the sermon *Deri Tuan Deos*, which means "On God the Lord."[5] Following the sermon on God, in his fourth sermon Wiltens preached on God's work in creating the heavens and the earth. In the fourth sermon he went into some detail in talking about the Genesis story of creation.

Wiltens' third and fourth sermons covered a similar topic of God's works in creation. The third sermon functioned as general introduction to his theological explication, and in this sermon he explained the doctrine of creation. He then revisited the same topic in the fourth sermon. These two sermons are two completely different sermons, however, the main content of the two sermons is not very different. In both sermons he spoke about the eternity of God and[6] the power of God in creation, especially on the fact that God created out of nothing.[7] In both sermons Wiltens also summarized the Genesis 1 story of the six days of creation.[8] Wiltens' theological explications on the doctrines of the Reformed church continued with his

---

5. Wiltens, *Maleysche Predicatien*, 22.
6. Compare Wiltens, *Maleysche Predicatien*, 1 and 33.
7. Compare Wiltens, *Maleysche Predicatien*, 3 and 33.
8. Compare Wiltens, *Maleysche Predicatien*, 4, 35, and 36.

The Sermons of Wiltens and Danckaerts

view of creation and providence in the fifth and sixth sermons. From there he went on to the explanation of attributes of God, particularly in connection with God's works in creation and providence. The topic of God's sovereignty was covered in his eighth sermon.

In the ninth sermon Wiltens took a somewhat different approach than what he did in the first eight sermons. While still preaching on God's sovereignty as a continuation of the topic of first his eighth sermons, in this sermon he retold the history of Israel in Egypt. His ninth through twelfth sermons covered much of the book of Exodus. Even though Wiltens did not cite any biblical passages in these sermons, he told the history of the Isrealites in Egypt beginning with the bitterness of slavery, through the birth of Moses and the exodus story in such a way that the stories could function as a substitute of parts of the book of Exodus for the people. These sermons were Wilten's way to set the stage for his last two sermons, namely his explication of the Ten Commandments. The approach that Wiltens took gives us an impression that he wanted to place the sermons on the Ten Commandments as the pinnacle of all his sermons. Perhaps he thought that the sermons on the Ten Commandments should and would be the most important ones for the audience to remember. It is rather surprising, however, that the collection of sermons ended abruptly without a good conclusion. The second part of the fourteenth sermon ended with the explication on the sixth commandment. The sermon ends with an "Amen" as all his other sermons did, giving an indication that the sermon was complete. The title of the published work also indicates that there are fourteen sermons in the series. In addition, in the preface Heurnius did not mention or explain why the collection of sermons only ended with the sixth commandment.

Even though his sermons were heavy with doctrine, Wiltens was very careful in crafting his words for the people. His knowledge and fluency in Malay was commendable. At the beginning of every sermon Wiltens would review the topic that he had covered the previous Sunday. This step was necessary considering that most of the indigenous people in the East Indies were new to the Reformed faith, and they needed to see the continuity from one sermon to the next. By reviewing the previous Sunday's sermon Wiltens reminded the congregation the main points of his sermon and then he would continue to provide the congregation with new teaching. As these sermons were circulated later and read by non-ordained church workers such as the comforters of the sick and school teachers during church services in remote villages, the continuity of thought and teaching that Wiltens provided would be preserved.

Wiltens started his series of sermons with an explication of God's eternal nature. He showed God's sovereignty by pointing out that the eternal God is not limited by anything and that God does not depend on anything.[9] He particularly pointed out that God's work in creating the heavens and the earth out of nothing is the best demonstration of his sovereignty and power.[10] Wiltens spoke with ease of the biblical creation story without ever citing any biblical verses. He did not even tell his audience that the story of creation was written in the book of Genesis. He simply told the people and expected the listeners to accept what he said as truth. In his sermon delivery, however, Wiltens showed good understanding of the daily lives of his audience. He used illustrations that he took from the day-to-day activities of the people in the East Indies. For instance, in showing that God always shows providential care for all creation, he said that God is like the captain of a ship. As a person who had sailed from Batavia to Ambon, he was sure that most of the people in the archipelago knew how a captain would work on a ship, namely, providing leadership, guidance and control over the entire crew and what happens on the ship. He used this illustration to show how God is always in control, just like a captain is in control of his ship all the time.

The bulk of Wiltens' sermons focused on the teaching of fundamental doctrines of the Reformed church. There is hardly any practical application that he would call the people to do in their daily lives. Through the way he delivered his sermons one gets the impression that his main intention was to lay the groundwork for providing the people with doctrinal teaching and knowledge of theology rather than transformation of daily conduct from a pre-Christian or non-Christian way of life to a Christian way of life. Perhaps he expected that with proper knowledge of the content of Christianity the people would experience change gradually. Considering that Wiltens' collection of sermons was the first one to be circulated in the East Indies, we could understand that by providing these sermonss to the people in the East Indies he implanted the basic teachings of the Reformed faith in the first two decades of the presence of the Dutch in the archipelago.

Wiltens moved from one topic to the next swiftly. He often told biblical stories in the sermon without quoting any single biblical passage. He did

---

9. Wiltens, *Maleysche Predicatien*, 2.
10. Wiltens, *Maleysche Predicatien*, 3.

The Sermons of Wiltens and Danckaerts

this quite possibly because the people still did not have Bible in their vernacular. This situation became exciting when he explained the nature of the Scripture in his second sermon. It is worth noting that by the time Wiltens preached this sermon, the people in the East Indies still did not have a Bible in their own language. Yet Wiltens found no difficulty in preaching to the people about the Bible as God's special revelation. In establishing the Reformed understanding of special revelation, he pointed out that we know God personally through the Sacred Scriptures.[11] In introducing how human beings could know God and his works, Wiltens simply stated that humans know all of these from the Sacred Scriptures. He explained the nature of Scripture as letters and books that were written a long time ago that contain foretelling of events that would happen in the future. In this explanation he mostly focused on the prophetic nature of the Scripture. In order to argue the truthfulness and the reliability of the Scriptures he pointed out that the fulfillment of prophecy, miracles and the antiquity of the writings of the Scriptures as the proof that the Scriptures are dependable.[12] Believing that the Scriptures are the words of God, he also emphasized that the words of the Scriptures have the power to change people and to make them righteous and thus to prevent eternal damnation in hell.[13] It is clear in his sermon that Wiltens saw the Scriptures as the living words of God, and these living words have the power to transform people and therefore to bring salvation. It is very interesting to see how Wiltens was arguing for the truthfulness of the Scriptures while the indigenous people still did not have the Bible in their own language. In a way his sermons functioned as the Bible for the people. Even though the people did not have copies of Bible in the language that they understood, they could rely on what he told the people and thus his words became the substitute for the Bible.

In the context of the Dutch's efforts to colonize the East Indies, what Wiltens did to a certain extent demonstrated the attitude of the colonists to the colonized people. Wiltens represented authority. He had the authority as a minister. At the same time he also had the authority as the new power that came to the archipelago. In his efforts to bring the teaching of the Reformed church to the people, he exercised this authority whether he realized it or not. The very fact that he did not quote biblical verses when he spoke about stories in the Bible and biblical doctrine indicated that he

11. Wiltens, *Maleysche Predicatien*, 11.
12. Wiltens, *Maleysche Predicatien*, 12–13.
13. Wiltens, *Maleysche Predicatien*, 16.

was fully confident that he did not need to base his sermons on the biblical text. We have reasons to believe that he was sincere in his ministry and his sermons demonstrated that he had an excellent knowledge of the Bible. In addition, as an ordained minister in the Dutch Reformed church, he was already given the rights and privilege to preach. Thus, this means that the Reformed church in the Netherlands acknowledged his credibility as a preacher. But at the same time we also see that he represented the power of the Dutch people and the VOC. Therefore, he was comfortable in preaching without basing his sermons on any biblical text.

Wiltens consistently used the Portuguese word *Deos* for God. He explained that the Malay people did not have their own word for God. He recognized that the Arabic people used the term *Allah* to refer to God. He said that *Allah* is equal to any other name for God in other languages. The Dutch people used the word *Godt* and the Portuguese used *Deos*. He further said that because the Portuguese word had been used very widely throughout the archipelago, he chose to follow the custom, and therefore he used the word *Deos* to refer to God.[14] In the sermon he also reminded the people that even though human beings use human words to refer to God, it does not mean that God is limited by the human mind, because God is eternal and above everything else in the universe.

Wiltens' last two sermons covered the first six of the Ten Commandments. The thirteenth sermon dealt with the first four commandments. The last sermon in the series focused on the fifth and sixth commandments. As he preached on the first six commandments, Wiltens put more concrete applications in what the people must do in order to fulfill the commandments. Worship of the true God became the focus of his last two sermons. In the thirteenth sermon he kept reminding the people that because God is the only true God who created the heavens and the earth, Christians must always worship God alone, fear him and pray only to him.[15] As he explained the second commandment, "You shall not make an image . . . ," he delivered a message that directly addressed the indigenous people's daily experience with idol worship. He sternly criticized traditional practices of the Ambonese that dealt with various kinds of spiritism. He also criticized certain syncretistic practices in which the Ambonese took their traditional practice of worshipping a certain spirit but then readdressed the worship to God as though God was the substitute of the spirits that the people had

---

14. Wiltens, *Maleysche Predicatien*, 22.
15. Wiltens, *Maleysche Predicatien*, "De Derthiende Predicatie," passim.

been worshiping prior to their coming into contact with Christianity. He explicitly said that the true God of the Bible is not the same as these spirits. He insisted that God only accepts worship and prayer that is directed to him and done in the way that he wants.[16] He described idol worship as the deeds that only crazy people do. He used the term *orang gila* to refer to these idol worshippers. In Malay, the phrase connotes a person who has lost his or her mind.[17]

In explaining the meaning of the third commandment Wiltens showed that swearing constitutes blasphemy.[18] He said that he often heard many people swear using the holy name of God. He reminded his audience that swearing is against the second commandment. He also reminded the people that using hard words that people often direct to God as they suffer is also sin against this commandment. He recognized that people might not mean it when in pain they cry out against God, but still he thought that this is a trespass against this commandment.[19]

The fourteenth sermon, which was on the fifth commandment, could serve as a very good example of how Wiltens brought home hierarchy and power to the people. In line with the Reformed tradition, he showed that the command to honor one's father and mother goes beyond honoring one's biological parents. This commandment, he insisted, means to honor those who have authority above us, including head of the clan, head of the city and king of the country.[20] Ultimately, he said, God has given the authority to people who are above us, and this authority also means power to punish those who do wrong.[21] Because the power that leaders have comes from God, he further explained, leaders must represent God and act justly.[22] However, he also reminded the people that even in the case when a leader does not act justly and the people under the power of the leader disliked him, there is no reason for the people not to respect the leader, because honoring leaders is God's command to the people.[23]

---

16. Wiltens, *Maleysche Predicatien*, 142.
17. Wiltens, *Maleysche Predicatien*, 142.
18. Wiltens, *Maleysche Predicatien*, 144.
19. Wiltens, *Maleysche Predicatien*, 144.
20. Wiltens, *Maleysche Predicatien*, 149.
21. Wiltens, *Maleysche Predicatien*, 150.
22. Wiltens, *Maleysche Predicatien*, 151.
23. Wiltens, *Maleysche Predicatien*, 152.

One practical application that Wiltens invited the people to do in fulfilling the call to honor those who have authority above others is to be thankful and to express gratitude for their hard work. He pointed out that kings and leaders maintain the stability of the kingdom or region, enforcing law and providing protection for the people so that they can live peacefully. Therefore, he thought that it was only appropriate that people express their gratitude to their leaders.[24] He singled out teachers as a group of leaders to whom the people should show their gratitude. He talked about teachers as those who tirelessly work with their hands and also with their minds. In his opinion, teachers are busy using their intelligence so that they cannot take up any additional job to add to their earning. He called the people to respect and honor teachers specifically, because teachers provide leadership and teaching but they do not earn as much as others.[25] Wiltens' last remark in this sermon was his way of calling the people to respect and honor church workers. They were not highly paid, and those who were sent to the East Indies had sacrificed so much for the work of the church. Therefore, it was only fitting that they receive respect because of their work.

A sermon based on the fifth commandment delivered by a minister who was one of the colonizers might have been difficult for the colonized people to accept. In the context of a shifting of power from the local leaders to the colonizers, the indigenous people might have had significant questions to ask. Was the minister really speaking God's words, or was he trying to instill in the minds of the people unquestioning obedience to the new power? Was this sermon a faithful explication of God's message, or was this propaganda? Despite the fact that Wiltens had sacrificed his comfortable life in the Netherlands to go to the islands of the Moluccas, he was still one of the Dutch people who wanted to monopolize the trade of spices from the archipelago. In this sermon Wiltens did not explicitly say that the people should look at the Dutch as their leader and therefore honor the Dutch, but in reality, the VOC took over power from the local kings and regents all throughout the archipelago. By extension, therefore, the call to honor their leaders meant that the people must honor the Dutch authority. In the last part of his last sermon he called people's attention to stay away from murder. He said that because God has given people their lives, they must respect other people's live, therefore, murder is forbidden. He even told the

---

24. Wiltens, *Maleysche Predicatien*, 155.
25. Wiltens, *Maleysche Predicatien*, 155.

people that they must do what is good for other people, even when those people have done wrong to them.[26]

Sebastian Danckaerts' Sermons

Sebastian Danckaerts was born in 1593. His first arrival in the East Indies was at Bantam, where he became minister in 1616–1617. He later became minister in Ambon between 1618 and 1622 and in Batavia between 1624 and 1634. He died in Batavia in 1634.[27] While he was in Ambon he delivered a series of sermons in Malay which he then circulated. There are fourteen sermons on the Lord's Prayer and one on Easter found in the collection of Danckaerts' sermons.[28]

Like those of Wiltens, Danckaerts' sermons are also characterized by a strong emphasis on knowledge of Reformed doctrine and a call for the people to follow the teaching of the Reformed church. Danckaerts did not spend time in explaining the Bible. In the series of fourteen sermons on the Lord's Prayer, not even once did he cite the biblical passage in which the Lord's Prayer is found. Instead, he seemed to be assuming that the Ambonese were familiar with the Lord's Prayer. As Danckaerts preached to people who were relatively new to the teachings of Reformed Protestantism, his approach to the delivery of his sermons carried the characteristics of evangelistic efforts. He often compared the practice of pagan religions he saw in Ambon and surrounding islands and the true worship of the God of the Bible. He never hesitated to criticize pagan religions and in so doing he urgently called people to leave their old religions and come to the Protestant faith. It is necessary for us to note here that even though Danckaerts and other ministers that were sent to the East Indies in the earlier part of the seventeenth century would not fit within the modern category of missionaries, these ministers truly did the work of evangelization.

Danckaerts approached his evangelistic effort in his sermons by way of applying the Reformed view of creation, sin and redemption. He opened his first sermon on the Lord's Prayer by showing how sinful all people are. The biggest sin that he pointed out is the sin of idolatry. Like Wiltens he

---

26. Wiltens, *Maleysche Predicatien*, 159.
27. End, *Ragi Carita*, 252.
28. Danckaerts, "Conciones Malaicae in Ecclesia Amboynensi habitae" (1619, unpublished manuscripts). Hereafter: Dancaerts, "Sermon [number]," followed by page number of the manuscript.

showed the Ambonese that their land was full of idol worship. Worshipping idols, he said, was a sign that human beings realized they needed help from a being that was bigger than them, but they could not come up with the right idea of the worship of the true God.[29] Danckaerts' thought here perfectly reflects Calvin's view that idolatry is a strong proof that every human person has the sense of divinity in them. Calvin believed that no single person would be willing to place themselves below an object and worship that object if people did not have the idea of God.[30] For Calvin this sense of the divine is embedded in the fact that human beings are created in God's image. Calvin insisted that human beings do not learn the sense of divinity through school or formal education, but already have it since being in the womb. Because of human sinfulness, Calvin further explained, the sense of divinity becomes twisted, and human beings fall into their own traps and fail to worship the true God, worshipping instead "a figment and a dream of their own heart."[31]

Even though Danckaerts did not explicitly use the term "sense of divinity" as Calvin did, his thoughts were perfectly in line with that of Calvin. He simply said that all humans know within themselves what is right and what is wrong. In addition, human beings also know how to help others and how to seek help from others. But when it comes to the most ultimate help that pertains to the spiritual needs that are bigger than what human beings can handle, they do not seek help from the true God, but instead they create their own idols.[32] He called all idol worshipers *cafir*. This Malay word, derived from Arabic, signifies a person who does not believe in God. Danckaerts used this word for all the Gentiles and people who prayed to the wrong gods and asked for help and blessings from inanimate objects of gold, silver, wood or stone. He called idol worshippers stupid, because they believe these inanimate objects have power and ability to act, while in fact they are just part of the created order.[33] In contrast to these idols, Danckaerts showed that the true God of the Christian faith is the creator of heaven and earth, and therefore God is above all things, human and natural. This true God is the only one that is worthy to be worshiped and who can truly provide help for his people. In addition, emphasizing one of the

29. Danckaerts, "Sermon 1," 1.
30. Calvin, *Institutes of the Christian Religion*, 1.3.1.
31. Calvin, *Institutes*, 1.4.1.
32. Danckaerts, "Sermon 1," 1.
33. Danckaerts, "Sermon 1," 1.

fundamental teachings of Reformed Protestantism, Danckaerts stated that God has created human beings to be his image bearers and has subjected the rest of creation under human care and authority, therefore, it is wrong for humans to worship objects or animals that are in reality lower in dignity than humans.[34]

In the same breath in which he criticized pagan religions, Danckaerts also criticized Ambonese Christians who claimed to be worshipping the true God, praying to the true God and confessing the Christian faith but in reality were not worshipping the true God. Danckaerts might have had the Roman Catholics in mind. Even though he did not mention them by name, his criticism of how some Ambonese pretended to worship the true God and called themselves Christians but were not truly Christians brings us to conclude that he was addressing the Roman Catholics.

In his sermons, as he did in translating the Heidelberg Catechism, Danckaerts mostly used the Portuguese term *Deos* to refer to God. At times, however, in order to teach the new Protestants a deeper biblical understanding of God, from time to time Danckaerts used the name *Jehovah* to refer to God. He did not take the time to explain to his listeners the Hebrew origin of the name, most likely because he knew that the Ambonese were not familiar with the Hebrew Bible. However, his use of the name *Jehovah* indicated an effort to bring his listeners to closer commonality with more informed Christians from the Western world. For instance, in his second sermon on the Lord's Prayer, after showing that the only true God who is worthy of worship is the Lord and Master whom he called *Deos*, he stated that the name of this God is *Jehovah*, the only one God who is the Creator and Provider of the entire universe.[35] By showing that the name of God is *Jehovah*, Danckaerts brought his listeners closer to the Hebrew Bible, even in the time when the Bible was not yet made available to the people in their native language, and when the people still did not have sufficient historical knowledge of the Bible.

While he was strong in his effort to bring the people to the knowledge of the theological teaching of the Reformed faith, Danckaerts appealed to the hearts and the minds of his audience kindly and gently. His sermons, as I already indicated above, carried some characteristics of evangelistic preaching that we would find in the later time. After showing that the God of the Bible, *Deos* or *Jehovah*, was the only true God worthy to be

---

34. Danckaerts, "Sermon 1," 2.
35. Danckaerts, "Sermon 2," 3.

worshiped, he told his audience that this God calls the people to come to him in the sweetness of his heart, because God does not want his children to wander away and worship other gods, or even to worship angels, because angels are also God's creatures.[36] The love and sweetness of God's heart, he further stated, was demonstrated through the death and resurrection of Jesus, because God's anger at humans' sins had been appeased through the sacrifice that Jesus made. Then, in a very sympathetic and gentle statement that would be fitting in a nineteenth-century evangelistic campaign, Danckaerts said that Jesus Christ, the beloved Son of God, our Lord, had endured suffering and the punishment from God on the cross because of the depth of our sin. Then he ended his sermon with a clear calling for the people to worship, honor and obey God and only God.[37]

Danckaerts showed that prayer is both privilege and obligation. He stated that only human beings can pray to God. Animals do not have the need to be connected to God and therefore animals do not pray.[38] This was a concept he borrowed from Calvin.[39] At the same time, Danckaerts said that prayer is also an obligation for all Christians, because God's people must show gratitude to God for everything that God has done for them, especially in the great work of redemption. He emphasized the need for Christians to pray constantly, while at the same time he criticized the Ambonese who only prayed sporadically. He noted that some Ambonese, even though they confessed to be Christians, only prayed once every month or two.[40] What he was criticized there, he further clarified, were the people who were reluctant to go to church to worship even though these people confessed to be Christians. He then tried to shame these people by pointing out that the *gentio*, the non-Christians, watched their every move, and those who professed to be Christians but rarely went to pray and worship God failed to be good witnesses to their non-Christian neighbors.

One of the fundamental doctrines of the Reformed faith that Danckaerts instilled in the minds of the people was the power of prayer. He often stated that Christians must pray earnestly and correctly because it was what Jesus taught his disciples to do. He also emphasized that true prayer has power, and through their prayers God's people receive protection against

36. Danckaerts, "Sermons 2," 4.
37. Danckaerts, "Sermon 2," 4.
38. Danckaerts, "Sermon 3," 5.
39. Calvin, *Institutes*, 1.14.20, 1.16.16.
40. Danckaerts, "Sermon 3," 6.

the enemy, the devil. In the end, he stated that true prayer brought blessings in their lives.[41] This emphasis demonstrated how Danckaerts weaved doctrinal teaching and application in his sermons. While strongly building the people's theological knowledge of the significance of prayer, he also showed that praying would bring benefits in their daily lives.

Danckaerts cited the text of the Lord's Prayer in the fourth of the fourteen sermons that he used as elaborate explication of the prayer. He took the shorter version of the prayer, omitting the final sentence, "for thine is the kingdom and the power and the glory forever."[42] Danckaerts translated the prayer into Malay as follows:

> *Bappa cami, nang adde de langit namma-mou jadi poudji, alam mou datang pada cami, candhati-mou jadi begitou de dunja, begeimanna de surga. Redjiki cami derre saharihari, bri hari ini pada cami, lagi ampon dosa cami, begaimanna cami ampon capada siappa salla pada cami, jangan tsjoba pada cami pon lepascan cami derri djahat samoa.*[43]

In this sermon Danckaerts did not make any mention of the text of the Lord's Prayer that had already been printed and published by Ruyl in his *Sovrat ABC* of 1611. Danckaerts' sermons were delivered in 1619, about eight years after the *Sovrat ABC* went into print. A closer look at the *Sovrat ABC* reveals that the text of the Lord's Prayer in the small pamphlet followed the longer version of the prayer and that there were significant differences in the way the prayer was translated, which I will discuss later. The fact that Danckaerts did not mention the text in the *Sovrat ABC* may indicate that the pamphlet did not reach the audience to whom Danckaerts preached his sermons. This also raises the question of whether or not Danckaerts had access to the *Sovrat ABC*. Had Danckaerts had the small catechism book in his possession, one would expect that he would at least mention the existence of the other translation. Furthermore, if Danckaerts had the pamphlet in his possession, one would also expect that he would have eliminated complications by just using the text of the prayer in the *Sovrat ABC*. It would be too confusing to the new Protestants in the East Indies to have to follow two different translations of the same prayer with a slightly different length. Considering these issues, I conclude that

---

41. Danckaerts, "Sermons 3," 6.
42. Danckaerts, "Sermon 4," 8.
43. Danckaerts, "Sermon 4," 8.

Danckaerts could very well have been unfamiliar with the *Sovrat ABC* at the time when he delivered these sermons.

The *Sovrat ABC* translated the Lord's Prayer as follows:

> *Bappa hamba jang berdoudouck cadalam surga, berulcadoes manjady nama moe, hoccuman moe mendatangy, candahac moe mendjady de atas boemy seperty de dalam, sorga, beryla hamba moe macannan sedecala hary, mack beramponla doesa kyta, seperty, kyta berampon akan jang bersalah kepada hamba / d'jang-an berhenter kyta kapada fael seytan, macka pon mohoonla kyta dary pada yblis, carna toean ampoenja hocouman, daen cawassahan, daen berbassaran, dary sacarang lalou ka cakal. Amin.*[44]

Compared to the translation of the prayer in *Sovrat ABC*, Danckaerts' translation is more straightforward. He tried to make the translation to the point and his sentences were relatively shorter. Conciseness seemed to be the reason why he chose to take the shorter version of the prayer. Danckaerts seemed to be making an effort to help his audience understand the prayer without taking too much time to explain the concept. Ruyl, on the other hand, in translating the prayer was willing to use longer sentences and metaphors because he seemed to try to make the concept translatable to the people.

Danckaerts used the word *langit* to translate "heaven" while Ruyl used *sorga*. For Danckaerts, the employment of the word *langit*, which could mean the heavens or sky, or also heaven, fit within his overall focus of teaching his audience. To point to *langit* as the place where God dwells simply showed the Ambonese that God is above everything in this world because he does not reside in the world. Even though Danckaerts used *sorga* to refer to where God is in other parts of his sermons, the way he used *langit* at the beginning of the Lord's Prayer indicates that he wanted to point out the difference between God and the rest of the created order.

Unlike Ruyl, who translated the possessive pronoun "our Father" in the singular form *bapa hamba*, which literally means "my Father," Danckaerts stayed faithful to the original pronoun "our." Danckaerts also seemed to show more alignment with the Reformed tradition. The Heidelberg catechism question and answer 119 clearly uses the pronoun "our" in the prayer. In his *Institutes* Calvin also emphasized the significance of the word "our" to show that prayer is a communal enterprise and that God is the God

---

44. Ruyl, *Sovrat ABC*, A4v.

of all his people. Thus, according to Calvin, when we pray, we pray together with all believers.[45]

Danckaerts was more to the point than Ruyl in translating the second phrase in the prayer, "hallowed be thy name." Danckaerts translated the phrase as *namma-mou jadi poudji*, which literally means "your name be praised." In translating this phrase Danckaerts seemed to take liberty in transmitting the concept rather than being technical about language. The very basic meaning of this phrase is to praise God for who he is. The Malay word *poudji* means to praise. To "hallow" the name of God is to praise him, and thus Danckaerts' translation satisfies the intention of the prayer. Ruyl, on the other hand, took the more literal translation by using the Malay word *ulcadoes*, meaning "holy." The same term was commonly used to refer to the Holy Spirit as *R'uah Ulcadoes* in Danckaerts' translation of the Heidelberg Catechism.[46] Therefore, in employing the word *ulcadoes* Ruyl wanted to emphasize the holiness of the name of God. While Ruyl's translation is technically closer to the original language of the Bible, Danckaerts' translation would have been easier for the people in the East Indies to understand because praising the name of God would be an easier concept for the people to grasp than making the name of God holy.

The translations of "thy kingdom come" presents us with very interesting differences between the two men's look at the prayer. Danckaerts employed the Malay word *alam*, which he explained in his dictionary as having two meanings. The first meaning he described as *de gantsche werelt van de hemel ende aerde*,[47] or "the whole world from heaven to the earth." In the dictionary Dancaerts further explained that the word *alam* can also mean *een begryp van sekere landen*,[48] "the understanding of a particular land." He provided an example for the use of the second definition as *radja itou pounja alam*, which means "the land of that particular king" or "the kingdom of the king." Thus, when he translated the phrase "thy kingdom come" Danckaerts took the second definition of the word and applied that to God's kingdom. It would be wrong for one to consider that Danckaerts took the first definition of *alam*, namely the natural world, to show what the prayer means.

---

45. Calvin, *Institutes*, 3.20.38.
46. Danckaerts, *Heidelberg Catechism*, question and answer 53.
47. Wiltens and Danckaerts, *Vocabularium*, 69.
48. Wiltens and Danckaerts, *Vocabularium*, 70.

The Way to Heaven

Ruyl translated the phrase "thy kingdom come" as *houccouman mou mendatangi*. In the dictionary, Danckaerts translated the word *hoccoum* as *rechten* or *ordeelen*,[49] which means "law." Thus, in employing this word to translate the phrase, Ruyl took the liberty of looking at God's kingdom as the sphere where the rule or the law of God is present. Quite likely Ruyl wanted to show the people of the East Indies that whenever God's kingdom comes, his rules and law must also be obeyed. However, by not pointing to the presence of the kingdom of God and only to the rule and law of God, Ruyl may have depicted a stern and strict God who is only concerned about regulations. Danckaerts' translation provided a better understanding of God who, even though he is the king of the universe, has his kingdom also on earth. Danckerts' use of the word *alam* could also play double duty, showing that while God is not restricted by the created order, *alam* or "nature," the created order indeed belongs to God, and therefore the kingdom of God is also present in the world.

Another significant difference between Danckaerts' and Ruyl's translations is observable in their translations of "give us this day our daily bread." Danckerts used the Malay word *redjiki* to translated "bread." In his dictionary he defined the word as *noot drust van lijf-tocht en ein't het generael alles wat diet tot onderhoutdes lichaems*.[50] *Redjiki* is what people need for the maintenance of their lives. This translation shows us that Danckerts considered "bread" as the necessary sustenance for people's lives. Instead of literally translating the word "bread" into Malay, Danckaerts chose to explain the significance of bread in people's lives. Because the people of the East Indies did not depend on bread as their daily sustenance, Danckaerts did not seem to see the need for a word-for-word translation. Therefore, the employment of *redjiki* made better sense for him in showing that the petition brings the people to God to ask for their daily sustenance, beyond just food for the body. Ruyl, on the other hand, chose to use the word *macannan*, which refers to food in general. By choosing the word *macannan* Ruyl used a more literal translation even though he did not use the exact word for "bread." Food is still more general than bread, but by choosing a term for food to translate "bread" Ruyl still kept closer to the biblical text. However, Danckaerts' translation could be seen as closer to the intended message of the text, because the petition does not just mean asking for physical food, but asking for God's blessings and God's provision of all the

49. Wiltens and Danckaerts, *Vocabularium*, 89.
50. Wiltens and Danckaerts, *Vocabularium*, 106.

necessary things in life. Thus, the Malay word *redjiki* captures the meaning of the petition better.

Ruyl brought the prayer to the personal level instead of communal when he employed the first-person singular pronoun *hamba* in the petition. As in the beginning of the prayer, where he used the word *Bapa hamba* for "our Father," he translated the petition as *Beryla hamba moe macannan*. This effort of personalizing the prayer might have helped the new Christians in the East Indies to think that in prayer they were entering into God's presence personally and individually. The choice to use *hamba* fit with the general tone of the petition, since the word is also commonly used to refer to oneself when the person speaks to another person of much higher rank. The word could also mean a slave or a servant. Thus, *hamba* has the connotation of a lowly servant speaking and pleading to her master asking for help. Ruyl's use of *hamba* at the beginning of the Lord's Prayer and in this petition captured the relationship between God and human beings, even though it lost the communal aspect that prayer brings for the entire people.

The translations of the last petition, "lead us not into temptation but deliver us from evil," present another unique difference between the two men's views of the petition. Danckaerts used the more direct and straightforward translation. He used the Malay word *tsjoba*, which is the direct translation of "temptation." He translated "evil" into Malay as *djahat*. In so doing, Danckaerts produced short, straightforward phrases to translate the petition. Ruyl took a more indirect path. He translated "evil" into Malay as *fael seytan*, or "the nature of Satan." Through this translation we can see that for Ruyl tempting or temptation was the nature or the character of Satan. Therefore, in translating the petition he provided some interpretation that the petition actually focused on the fact that temptation only came from Satan's nature. The one praying is then led into asking to be delivered from the nature of Satan. Ruyl translated the petition to be delivered from evil as *mohoonla kyta dari pada yblis*, or "free us away from Satan." What catches attention in this translation is Ruyl's use of *yblis* for the word "evil." In his dictionary Danckaerts defined *yblis* as *den duyvel*,[51] "the devil." By using *yblis* for "evil" Ruyl seemed to be presenting the idea that evil and the devil are actually one and the same. In so doing, Ruyl seemed to be representing an approach of translating the petition as "deliver us from the evil one." In this translation the request in the prayer for deliverance from the one who is evil.

---

51. Wiltens and Danckaerts, *Vocabularium*, 90.

The Way to Heaven

Even though Danckaerts' main focus in his sermons was the implantation of Reformed theological doctrines in the minds of the people, he still kept a preaching style that addressed the emotion and feeling of his listeners. In showing the love of God to his people, Danckaerts used an illustration that he took from the daily lives of the Ambonese. He reminded the people that a mother hen would spread her wings wide to protect her young when danger approached. This metaphor is rooted in the Bible, while at the same time it was also close to the daily experience of the Ambonese. He kept reminding the people that they had seen such an act of mother hens, and he told the people that God is much greater than a mother hen. If an animal can do such thing for her young, God can protect and save his people far more than any creature can.[52] Therefore, he encouraged the people to come to God asking for help in time of need, because God listens to their cry.

The fatherhood of God, according to Danckaerts, is the one that binds all God's people as brothers and sisters in unity. His emphasis on God as "our Father" brought him to remind the people to treat each other well. He told the people that if they prayed together, as Christians, God was their Father, but if they still had enmity with each other they had failed to obey God's command. Calling God "our Father," he further stated, had the implication of forgiving others who have wronged us. Hence he stated that the Lord's Prayer calls all believers to be united with each other.[53] This is a true Christian teaching that all believers must follow. However, in the context of colonization period, one wonders how the colonized community would have thought of the colonizers. Would the people in the East Indies have readily embraced the message of Danckaerts' sermons? In the event that the colonizers treated them ill, while they all confessed the same Christian faith, would the colonized community have had the voice to tell the colonizers that they did not follow the teaching of the Christian faith that their own ministers earnestly taught?

In explaining the meaning of the phrase "hallowed be thy name," Danckaerts went over the meaning of God's revelation through his name. He showed that the name that God gives to the people is his revelation. God tells us who he is, and we must honor God and praise God for who he is. Through giving us his name God introduces himself to us. Danckaerts explained the meaning of God's revelation by showing that the fact

52. Danckarts, Sermon 4," 9.
53. Danckaerts, "Sermon 5," 11.

that God tells his people who he is makes it possible for the people to get in touch with God.⁵⁴ Just like human interaction, he continued to explain, our relationship with God is made possible because God has introduced himself to us. Thus, in a very simple way Danckaerts showed the people the very fundamental idea of God's revelation. He stated that the name *Jehovah* is God's own revelation to human beings, and God wants humans to know him intimately through this name. He reminded the people that the name *Jehovah* shows that God is "Lord of all lords and King of all kings."⁵⁵ The implication of knowing God intimately, he further explained, was that human beings must always come to God in repentance, because as King of all kings and Lord of all lords, God requires that all people who want to come to him must get rid of their sins.

As a devout Reformed minister, Danckaerts believed that the Bible is the special revelation from God to his people. In a rhetorical fashion he asked the question of how human beings could know God. He provided a simple answer, in a sentence that contained a mixture of Portuguese and Malay words: *Derri sagrada scriptura, attau becattahan dirinja*,⁵⁶ or in English: "[We know God from] the sacred scripture, or his own words." While Danckaerts' answer was a standard Reformed answer on the doctrine of special revelation, one might wonder of how the Ambonese would havea understood this statement. As I have discussed in the preceding chapter, the people still did not have the Bible in Malay until much later than Danckaert's time. The first Malay translation of the Gospel of Matthew, done by Ruyl, was published in 1629,⁵⁷ about ten years after Danckaerts delivered his series of sermons. Even though the Ambonese might have seen Dutch Bibles carried by these ministers, the people did not have the Bible in their language. Thus, like Wiltens' sermon before, Danckaerts sermon, especially his statement regarding Sacred Scripture as the special revelation of God, became a doctrinal statement that could be hard for the people to grasp. The people just had to accept whatever the minister told them. This is a good example to show that in the early years of the transplantation of Reformed Christianity in the East Indies, the Dutch ministers were more concerned with transplanting knowledge of the teachings of the Reformed

---

54. Danckaerts, "Sermon 6," 15.
55. Danckaerts, "Sermon 7," 17.
56. Danckaerts, "Sermon 7," 18.
57. Ruyl, *Het Evangelie naar Mattheus*.

church than with providing the people with close engagement of the Bible and letting the Bible become the foundation of the people's faith in God.

The goodness of God shines in his creation and also in his providential care of the universe he has made. Danckaerts moved further along in this doctrinal belief by showing the people that the beauty and goodness of creation comes out of God's goodness.[58] As he often did in his sermons, he used examples from the world around the people to help his audience understand. He showed that vegetables, fruit, animals and different seasons are good in themselves, but they are given to human beings so that they get the most benefit from the rest of creation.

From the goodness of creation, including the creation of human beings that was originally good, Danckaerts moved directly to the Reformed teaching of the human fall and sinfulness. Following the traditional view of original sin, he taught that even though created good, humans are now sinful.[59] Danckaerts believed that human heart is the center of the whole human being. He explained that the sinful nature of human beings lies at the heart as the core of all that is bad. In order to help the people understand, he likened the human hearts to rock, which love can no longer penetrate. In order to communicate the depth of the sinfulness of human nature, he used two Malay words: *tsjamar*, meaning "polluted," and *nadjijs*, meaning "ceremonially unclean." The word *nadjijs* was originally from Arabic, and among the Islamic people the word expressed any unclean person or object that a Muslim is not allowed to be near or touch. By employing these two words Danckaerts tried to teach the people that the sinful nature in human beings is a serious problem.

Like in the earlier part of the sermon, in this part Danckaerts went straight to the doctrinal teaching of the church without providing a biblical basis for his sermon. He mentioned the story of Adam and Eve and their fall into sin as the starting point of his explication on original sin as a given, without telling the people that the story is written in the book of Genesis. Considering that the people still did not have a Malay Bible, Danckaerts moved with ease in teaching the doctrine without seeing the need to refer to the biblical grounds for the doctrine.

Danckaerts explained that redemption is the work of the Holy Spirit. He believed that Holy Spirit could change human hearts that were hard as rock to be soft as flesh again. The Holy Spirit, he said, can wash an unclean

58. Danckaerts, "Sermon 6," 16.
59. Danckaerts, "Sermon 7," 18.

heart from all its impurity and pollution, just like fire can purify gold.[60] He also attributed the word of God as the word of the Holy Spirit that brings sinful human beings back to God. In so doing, he basically showed that God the Holy Spirit is actually the same as the Father and the Son. Redemption in Christ is the center of Danckaert's sermons. He first explained that the Son of God is one and same God as the Father, and together with the Holy Spirit they are the triune God.[61] In keeping with the underlying evangelistic tone that he consistently had throughout his sermons, Danckaerts emphasized that Jesus Christ is the only Savior for sinful humanity. He also put significant weight on the suffering of Jesus on the cross in the work of redemption to show the people that Jesus's sacrifice was not a trivial matter. The effect that he aimed at was that the people would respond by repenting from their sins and become faithful followers of Jesus.[62] The death and resurrection of Jesus delivered his people from sin. Danckaerts clearly said that because of the work of redemption that Christ completed, human beings are now freed from the bondage from Satan. Satan can no longer "drag us to do what is wrong, or what he likes, nor can he torture, turn us upside down, or trick us, or be our master and force us to bow down and worship him."[63]

Showing his complete adherence to the teaching of the Heidelberg Catechism, Danckaerts indicated that as the expression of gratitude to God for delivering his people from sin and the power of Satan, they must obey God in their lives. He elaborated the call to express gratitude to God by preaching on the Ten Commandments in his tenth sermon in the series of sermons on the Lord's Prayer.[64] This approach was unique in that he was able to include his thoughts on the Ten Commandments in the sermon on the Lord's Prayer. As we will see in the following section, Caron, who ministered a few decades later than Danckaerts, had a separate series of sermons on the Lord's Prayer and on the Ten Commandments. Because Danckaerts had been in the East Indies in the earlier decades of the seventeenth century, he seemed to want to be concise in his series of sermons. Hence he took the decision to abbreviate his thoughts on the Ten Commandments and packaged it inside his sermons on the Lord's Prayer.

60. Danckaerts, "Sermon 7," 19.
61. Danckaerts, "Sermon 9," 23.
62. Danckaerts, "Sermon 9," 24.
63. Danckaerts, "Sermon 9," 24.
64. Danckaerts, "Sermon 10," 26–29.

The Way to Heaven

Danckaerts tried to make his sermon speak to the very core of the Ambonese people and their daily religious lives. His sermons centered on the emphasis to know the fundamental teachings of the Reformed church and the constant call to repent and follow God's command. Danckaerts kept returning to the theme of God's goodness in creation, human sinfulness, redemption in Jesus Christ and a life of gratitude as redeemed people of God. Even though his sermons were intended to be the explication of the Lord's Prayer, one does not find much exposition on the prayer itself. Doctrine seems to have been the main guide for Danckaerts in constructing his sermons. Scripture functioned as an important background, but it stood only in the distance. Danckaerts did not spend a significant amount of time explaining Scripture. This was also true for his sermon for Easter Sunday. This sermon was inserted together with the sermons on the Lord's Prayer.[65] Even when he told the story of the death and resurrection of Jesus, he did not cite any biblical passages in the sermon. He constructed his sermon in such a way that he used it to reemphasize his message about Christ's redemptive work. He went into great detail in preaching that Jesus is truly divine and truly human, and that his death and resurrection are the best proof of this reality. Danckaerts' sermon reflects a theological perspective that is deeply seated in the Reformed tradition. However, considering his primary audience in the East Indies in the early seventeenth century, one wonders if such doctrine could have been completely understood by the people to whom the sermon was preached.

---

65. Danckaerts, "In Festum Pascuae," 38–40.

3

The Sermons of Franchois Caron as Further Reinforcement of the Establishment of Calvinism in the East Indies

Franchois Caron's Collection of Sermons

FRANCHOIS CARON JR. CAME to the East Indies long after the time of Wiltens and Danckaerts. His work, therefore, served as further advancement of the transplantation of Reformed Protestantism in the archipelago. His father, Franchois Caron Sr., was stationed in Hirado, Japan, as a VOC officer in Japan for twenty years. There he married a Japanese woman and had five surviving children. Franchois Caron Jr. was the middle child. The older Caron started his career as an assistant and a translator before he became the head of the VOC office in Hirado in 1639. In 1641 Caron Sr. moved to Batavia together with his wife and children. Caron publicly legalized the status of his five surviving children and gave them Dutch names and reared them as European Christians.[1] In 1643 Caron requested that the government of Batavia give him the certificate of legitimation for his five children. The Dutch government in Batavia gave Caron the legitimation to Daniel, Tobias, Franchois Jr., Patronella and Maria. The

---

1. Taylor, *Kehidupan Sosial di Batavia*, 76.

legitimation was based on the regulation made on September 26, 1643.² This was then confirmed by the law of legitimation December 18, 1646.³

Franchois Caron Sr. became the Director General of the VOC in Batavia on March 9, 1647.⁴ At that time Cornelis Van der Lijn had just succeeded Antonio Van Diemen as the Governor General of the VOC. Caron and Van der Lijn were close friends.⁵ Caron's tenure as Director General in Batavia coincided with the temporary stop on the war against Portuguese, following the truce of Goa in 1644. Therefore, his time in Batavia was uneventful when one sees it from military and political point of view. However, from the economic and administrative point of view, Caron's time was considered very fruitful.⁶

Franchois Jr was born in 1634 and went to Leiden to study theology for a few years. He later returned to the East Indies in 1660 and became a minister in Ambon for 14 years.⁷ Later on he was well known for his works in the Malay language and he preached using the local dialect of Ambon. In 1673 Franchois Jr. requested the permission to return to the Netherlands. He left Ambon for Batavia in 1674⁸ and eventually arrived in the Netherlands in 1675 together with his wife and children. He later became a preacher in Lexmonde, near Tiel.

As a minister in the East Indies Caron showed love and compassion to the indigenous people to whom he ministered. He worked hard to ensure that the people understood the teachings of Reformed Christianity so that they would live their daily lives according to their faith. This intention was clearly seen through his sermons. He tirelessly emphasized the need for the people to live out their faith and put their beliefs into action. When he returned to the Netherlands in 1675 he made an effort to publish his collection of sermons in Malay so that the non-ordained church workers in the East Indies could use the sermons in the worship services to help Christians in the archipelago to grow in their faith. In the dedicatory epistle

---

2. The decree of September 1643 was included in W. Wijnaendts van Reseandt's *De gezaghebbers der Oost-Indische Compagnieop*, 127.

3. Boxer, *True Description of the Mighty Kingdoms of Japan and Siam*, lxviii.

4. Boxer, *True Description*, xcv.

5. Boxer, *True Description*, xcvi.

6. Boxer, *True Description*, xcvii.

7. Caron wrote a brief summary of his ministry in Ambon in the preface of his published collection of sermons. See Caron, *Voorbeeldt des openbaeren Godtsdienst*, **4 recto.

8. Caron, *Voorbeeldt des openbaeren Godtsdienst*, **3 recto.

The Sermons of Franchois Caron as Further Reinforcement

to the directors of the VOC in Holland and Zeeland he explicitly stated his passion that the Christians in the Indies should be properly taught on Christian doctrine. He insisted that the people needed books in Malay and therefore he was thankful that the board of directors agreed to fund the publication of his sermons.[9] After a long process of preparation and printing, the work was finally completed in 1678. At the time of the completion of the work Caron was living in The Hague.[10] He also indicated that when he was still in Ambon, he saw that from time to time Christians in the islands of Ternate, Banda and other smaller islands in the region had already benefited from the Malay translations of significant Christian texts, including the small catechism, the Gospels and Genesis. These texts had been used in church worship services and also in schools.[11]

Caron also noticed that the schools got more benefit from the Malay texts than the church because by reading these texts, the school children could learn the basic foundation of Christianity at school. The churches in the remote villages did not receive as much benefit as the school children because the school teachers could only go to the remote villages four times a year to read the sermons to the believers there. In some cases, in the remotest islands of the region the school teachers could only visit the believers twice a year to administer the sacraments, to preach and to help the people learn Christianity.[12]

To the Christians of Ambon Caron stated that his printed sermons were intended as a fill in for his absence. He knew that many of his brothers and sisters in Ambon and surrounding islands had been waiting for a long time for the publication of his sermons. He explicitly thanked Anthony Hurt, the governor of Ambon, for his assistance in their publication.[13] He entitled the collection of sermons in Malay as *Tjeremin Acan Pegang Agamma*, or "Mirror to Hold the Religion." The Dutch title of this work is *Voorbeldt des Openbaeren Godtsdientsts*. Caron intended this work as a tool for the people to look at what they should believe, how they should lead their lives and how they must worship God.[14] He indicated that the sermons should be read in church on Sundays or other days of worship, in

---

9. Caron, *Voorbeeldt des openbaeren Godtsdienst*, *2 recto.
10. Caron, *Voorbeeldt des openbaeren Godtsdienst*, **4 verso.
11. Caron, *Voorbeeldt des openbaeren Godtsdienst*, *2 verso.
12. Caron, *Voorbeeldt des openbaeren Godtsdienst*, *3 recto.
13. Caron, *Voorbeeldt des openbaeren Godtsdienst*, **3 recto.
14. Caron, *Voorbeeldt des openbaeren Godtsdienst*, **3 verso.

the remote place where there were no ordained ministers residing. He intentionally wrote the sermons in Ambonese Malay so that the people could easily understand the content. He made the teaching and explanation in his sermons as simple as possible to help the people understand easier, because he realized that believers in the archipelago were still young in their faith. His ultimate goal was to stir the fire in the people's heart the fear of God and the love of Christ, because they had dedicated themselves to God in Christ when they were baptized. In so doing, he believed that the people would lead a righteous life, pray unceasingly to God, and in the end they would receive the wage of their labor, namely eternal life.[15]

The ultimate goal of eternal life was clearly the center of Caron's focus in his ministry. This was in line with the focus rest of his works as a minister. He wanted to show that Reformed Christianity was the only way to heaven. In the sermons he often argued that even though other religions also hoped to bring people to heaven, they all failed for they could not provide the true way to heaven. He kept emphasizing that Reformed Protestantism that he preached is the only key to open heaven's door, because it showed people the only way of salvation through Jesus Christ.

Caron often engaged himself in polemics against Islam and other religions. In the polemics he plainly described the contrast between the people's lives before coming to Christ and their current condition in Christ as a movement from sitting in the darkness of death, bounded by the ropes of Satan in the Islamic religion and paganism, into freedom in the kingdom of God's Son Jesus Christ, by way of the Gospel, the heavenly message and the power of the Holy Spirit.[16] In his sermons he often encouraged the people to send their children to school to be taught the foundations of the Christian faith. He understood that it was not easy for the Christians in the East Indies to proclaim their faith, because they lived among Islamic people and pagan believers.

While he aimed at reminding his readers and listeners to live out their faith through practical application of the sermons, Caron clearly had a keen theological foundation for his ministry and sermons. He considered Christians in Ambon his brothers and sisters, and in line with the Calvinistic faith that he held, he called the Ambonese Christians together with he himself the adopted children of God the Father, and they became brothers

---

15. Caron, *Voorbeeldt des openbaeren Godtsdienst*, **3 verso.
16. Caron, *Voorbeeldt des openbaeren Godtsdienst*, **3 verso.

and sisters because of the work of the older brother Jesus Christ.[17] He also showed care and love to the people, indicating that the fourteen years they were together when he was minister in Ambon were very fruitful years and that enjoyed the time when he could share the word of God with them. At the end of the preface he indicated that he looked forward to the end of time when Jesus would come for the second time and the sound of the trumpet would be heard, and they would see each other again and receive the crown as a reward from the Lord, the righteous judge. Here Caron was paraphrasing Paul's Letter to Timothy. At that time they would never be separated ever again.

The closing paragraph of Caron's preface exemplifies how he integrated strong biblical and theological teaching with contextualization and cultural awareness that was necessary to enable his readers and hearers in the East Indies to understand what he meant. As he already wrote in *De Wegh na den Hemel*, he used the Malay term *hari kjamat* as the free translation for the second coming of Christ.[18] He looked forward to the second coming of Jesus because it would be the wonderful time when they would be reunited in Christ and they would enjoy each other's company eternally. This reunification would be a part of the eternal blessedness that believers would enjoy when Jesus returns. In describing the crown that believers would receive as the reward and glory at the second coming of Christ, he used the Malay term *deystar-Radja*, meaning "the turban of a king."[19] This approach is clearly a contextual adaptation of the biblical imagery. He was aware that in the East Indies the tribal kings did not wear crowns like European kings did. He must have seen, and he knew that his audience understood, that kings in the East Indies wore a turban. This custom was clearly an influence of the Middle Eastern and Indian customs that were brought to the East Indies together with the arrival of Islam. In order to make his message understandable, Caron freely translated the word "crown" as *deystar-Radja*. This type of free translation was characteristic of Caron's work. This approach was also an indication that the communication of the Protestant concept and teaching relied on the existing terms and concept that were readily available in the experience of the people. Caron, as well as other

---

17. Caron used the Malay term *kaka* to describe Jesus' relationship with the people. In Malay, the word *kaka* literally means "older brother." Caron, *Voorbeeldt des openbaeren Godtsdienst*, **4 recto.

18. Caron, *Voorbeeldt des openbaeren Godtsdienst*, **4 recto.

19. Caron, *Voorbeeldt des openbaeren Godtsdienst*, **4 verso.

The Way to Heaven

Dutch ministers working in the East Indies, had to be willing to borrow concepts that were originated in other religious cultures and experience if he wanted to communicate his intention well.

There are forty sermons in the collection that Caron published. There are twelve sermons based on the Apostles' Creed, one sermon for each article, ten sermons on the Ten Commandments, and seven sermons on the Lord's Prayer, with one sermon on the opening statement, "Our Father who art in heaven," and six sermons on each of the petitions in the Lord's Prayer. Following this set of sermons are eight sermons for Feast Days, consisting of two sermons for Easter, one sermon for Pentecost, two sermons for Christmas and one sermon for New Year's Day. At the end of the collection there are three sermons for special services, namely one sermon for the anniversary of Fort Victoria in Ambon, a sermon for times of trouble and a sermon for thanksgiving. Like Wiltens' printed sermons, Caron's sermons were printed in quarto size, with double columns on each page. The length of each sermon wa approximately 2800–3000 words. When they are read each of these sermons would last 30–40 minutes. We have reasons to believe that Caron's sermons were widely used in the East Indies long after he returned to his fatherland. After the initial publication in 1678 they were reprinted in 1693 and then again in 1738.[20] In the research for this book I use the 1693 edition published by Paulus Matthysz.

While Caron's sermons were intended to help Christians in the East Indies to grow in their faith and knowledge of Christianity, to a certain extent they also functioned as a means to promote and strengthen the presence of the Dutch in the land. In other words, some of the sermons also functioned as propaganda for the goodness of the VOC. This effort was seen in the inclusion of the sermon for the celebration of the anniversary of the taking over of Fort Victoria in Ambon from the hands of the Portuguese.[21] The celebration of this victory was done every February 23. Caron entitled his sermon *Pen-ingatan deri ala Cota Victoria di Tanna Ambon, jang jadi pegang capada boulang Februario hari jang ca 23*, or in English, "Rememberance from the City Victoria in the Land of Ambon, Which is Celebrated on February 23."

Caron started the celebratory sermon with a reading from Psalm 18:46–47. The sermon was a clear exposition of David's praise to God because God has delivered him from his enemies. He reminded his audience

20. Landwehr, *VOC*.
21. Caron, *Voorbeeldt des openbaeren Godtsdienst*, Ff3 verso–Gg3 recto.

of how throughout his life David had seen the hands of God delivering him from his enemies. From his younger years to almost the end of his life, David had several enemies. Saul wanted to kill him. Then, after David became king in Jerusalem, his own son Absalom plotted against him. These were the two enemies that David had to face, and they were from within Israel. However, David also faced several attacks from enemies from outside Israel. When David was in confrontation with the Philistines, the Moabites and many other nations, Caron stated in his sermon, the fights were clearly fights between God's chosen people represented by David and the unclean people who were the enemies of God. The biblical passage that Caron cited at the beginning of the sermon used the Malay term *orang horgay*[22] to indicate these people. The Malay-Dutch dictionary that Sebastiaan Danckaerts and Caspar Wiltens developed in the earlier decades of the seventeenth century listed the term *horgay* to mean *een vreemdelinck* in Dutch.[23] It is interesting to see how Caron employed this passage, and especially the term *horgay* in the context of the sermon to commemorate the victory of the Dutch over the Portuguese in the battle over Fort Victoria. Caron explained that the *horgay* or the enemies of David over whom he was victorious were the Philistines, the Ammonites, the Moabites and the Jebusites. They were the descendants of Ham, one of Noah's sons. The Israelites, on the other hand, were the descendants of Shem, the chosen son of Noah.[24] Because David and the Israelites worshiped the true God, Caron explained, they were protected by God. These enemies of Israel were "foreigners," and more specifically they were foreigners because they were enemies of God. In Malay, Caron further stated, these people could also be called the *Hindou* people. In seventeenth-century Malay this term was used to indicate the Gentiles, the uncircumcised people. Caron used Paul's letter to the Ephesians (2:11–12) to explain that these *Hindou* people were the ones separated from the company of the chosen people of God, the children of Abraham.[25]

Like Danckaerts before him, Caron used the term *cafiri*, or "godless people," to describe these foreigners.[26] In the context of Caron's sermon that celebrated the triumph of the Dutch over the Portuguese, it was clear that

22. Caron, *Voorbeeldt des openbaeren Godtsdienst*, Ff4 folio 166.
23. Loderus, *Maleische Woord-Boek Sameling*, 89.
24. Caron, *Voorbeeldt des openbaeren Godtsdienst*, Ff4 folio 166.
25. Caron, *Voorbeeldt des openbaeren Godtsdienst*, fol. 166.
26. See discussion of Danckaerts' use of the term in chapter 3 above.

The Way to Heaven

Caron likened the Dutch to David and the Israelites, the ones to whom God had shown favor by way of driving away their enemies from their land. The text in Psalm 18 says that the foreigners have been defeated, they have lost heart and they come trembling from their stronghold. It is easy to make a parallel between the Dutch and the Israelites, over against the Gentiles and the Portuguese. The Malay translation of the psalm used the word *cota* for "stronghold."[27] In the Malay-Dutch dictionary, the term *cota* was defined as *casteel, vasticheyt vesten, ofte wallen*.[28] Fort Victoria in those days was called "Casteel Victoria." It was very easy for Caron to make a connection between the fall of the Portuguese and the trembling and defeat of the enemies of Israel. In the battle against the Portuguese, the Dutch gained significant victory, and the fort that used to be the stronghold of the Portuguese was then taken over by the Dutch, and the Portuguese must have trembled when they were defeated. By quoting the psalm that showed David's praise of God for his protection against his enemies, Caron likened the Dutch as the victorious Israelites. Therefore, in the annual celebration of the victory, the Dutch also invited the Ambonese to be joyful together with them in praising God for the victory.[29]

Caron took a very positive look at the victory of the Dutch over the Portuguese. He briefly included the historical event of the defeat in his sermon, with a special highlight of how easily van der Haghen took over Ambon. He attributed the victory to God.[30] Caron invited the Ambonese Christians to remember the event well, and also pointed out that the reason why they celebrated the event every year was to praise God for his unending kindness to his people. In this case, the people to whom God had been kind were the Dutch. And then he addressed the Ambonese who might be skeptical of the significance of the victory for them, considering that the victory belonged to the VOC and not to them, by saying that it was wrong for the Ambonese not to be joyful over the victory. He insisted that the celebration was beneficial for the Ambonese, because by driving out the Portuguese the Dutch had given the Ambonese a much better leader, one who is like a king with a kind heart. Citing reports that he heard from older natives of Ambon who experienced Portuguese rule, Caron stated that the

27. Caron, *Voorbeeldt des openbaeren Godtsdienst*, 165.
28. Loderus, *Maleische Woord-Boek Sameling*, 81.
29. Caron, *Voorbeeldt des openbaeren Godtsdienst*, 168.
30. Caron, *Voorbeeldt des openbaeren Godtsdienst*, 169.

Portuguese were people with great appetite for power and hard hearts, whereas the Dutch had ruled the land with kind heart, and more justice.[31]

Realizing that the Dutch came to the Moluccas with a main intention that was not too different from that of the Portuguese, Caron added that there was always the need for a leader that held the authority over the land. The leader would prevent wars and fights between groups of people. While he did not explicitly mention who should be such a leader, it is clearly implied that the Dutch came to the island to be the just ruler. He acknowledged that the Dutch came to Ambon to gain some fortune by collecting cloves and other expensive spices, just like what the Portuguese did. But then he defended the Dutch's presence on the island by stating that the Portuguese only wanted to take the wealth of the island, but the Dutch came to the island with the grace and mercy of God, because they brought the true Christian faith to the people. The Dutch had brought the most valuable treasure that was more than cloves, diamonds or pearls because they had brought the message of salvation to the people.

Caron further wrote that before the arrival of the Dutch the Ambonese were blind, as they walked in the darkness of their souls because they worshipped false gods made of wood, iron and stone as well as worshipping crocodiles, the sky, the earth, several spirits and even Satan. He first criticized the Islamic religion for teaching the people to worship false gods. Then, in his attack to the Portuguese, he stated that when they came to the island they brought Christianity, however, the kind of Christianity that the Portuguese brought was against the teaching of the word of God. In Malay, Caron called the Roman Catholic faith of the Portuguese as a religion that *batsydera sangat dengan surat Allah*, or "deeply wounded the letter [or the word] of God."[32] Then in parenthesis, as though mocking the teaching of the Portuguese, he added that as a source of water in a well, the Portuguese still needed to get water from a well of true teaching.[33] His attack of the Roman Catholicism that the Portuguese brought was bold. He criticized the Portuguese who introduced false gods of wood, iron and stone in the forms of wooden crosses and earthen statues of saints to be worshiped. Caron made it clear that it was only after van der Haghen arrived in Ambon that the true God was present among the people. Drawing from the historical event in which the Portuguese governor Gaspar de Melo opened the gate

---

31. Caron, *Voorbeeldt des openbaeren Godtsdienst*, 169.
32. Caron, *Voorbeeldt des openbaeren Godtsdienst*, 171.
33. Caron, *Voorbeeldt des openbaeren Godtsdienst*, 170.

of the fort and handed in the key to van der Haghen, Caron said that as the Portuguese had opened the gate of the fort, God also opened the door of the kingdom of heaven, enlightened the hearts of the people by way of the lights of the word of the Holy Spirit, and gave the gift of salvation in Jesus Christ through whom all people were justified. In order to be more inclusive and to sound less patronizing regarding the eternal salvation of all people, and not just that of the Ambonese, Caron switched his rhetorical tone and used a first-person plural inclusive pronoun *kitaorang* in the next part of his sermon. This Malay word means "all of us."[34]

Caron's sermon served as a good example of a blend of propaganda to support the Dutch's presence in the island and true Calvinistic theology and belief. It is clear that he considered the presence of the Dutch had been much better service to the Ambonese. The Dutch brought the true form of Christianity and because of the presence of the Dutch the people could come to know eternal salvation. Therefore, the Ambonese should be thankful to God—if not to the Dutch—for the gift of salvation. Caron must have fully understood that the VOC was there in the Moluccas to colonize. But because he was a servant of the VOC he had to serve his superiors and not say anything against them. At the same time, however, Caron was also a true Calvinist. He believed that salvation only came from God through Jesus Christ. He sufficiently expounded this truth in the sermon. He made it clear that together with the arrival of the Dutch God had opened the door to salvation. In this case the Dutch served as the messenger of the word of God. In line with the theology of Reformed Protestantism, he believed that is God the Holy Spirit who actually works out the salvation in the heart of every believer. In switching to the inclusive pronoun *kita orang* in the sermon, Caron showed his personal belief that he too was a sinner in the past. Even though he criticized pagan worship, the Islamic religion and Roman Catholicism, which did not do any good for the native Ambonese, he also included himself in the company of sinners who were to be destroyed in hell had God not provided salvation in Jesus Christ.

Caron ended the sermon with further demonstration of how God had brought goodness to the Ambonese. He showed how since the arrival of van der Haghen several ministers had come to the island. These ministers, he said, had preached, administered baptism and the Lord Supper, going from one village to another, visiting churches and teaching young children in schools. By the time Caron was in Ambon there were forty-three churches

---

34. Caron, *Voorbeeldt des openbaeren Godtsdienst*, 170.

and one school, with more than one thousand Protestants living in the island.³⁵ The works of the ministers had been a true testimony that God was good to his people. On the one hand he reminded the people that all praise must only be to God, not to these teachers and ministers, and not even to van der Haghen. But on the other hand he also called the people to thank the VOC for doing good deeds for the people. The VOC had been keeping the land well, Caron argued, and the company had also spent good amount of money to ensure that Christianity could flourish in the land by way of paying the ministers and school teachers, as well as sending books to the school for the children to learn. Therefore he encouraged the Ambonese to pray for the company so that God would always take care of the VOC who was the head or leader of the people.³⁶

Caron's Sermons on the Apostles' Creed

Caron's intention to provide doctrinal teaching to the Ambonese Christians was clearly demonstrated in his twelve sermons on the Apostles' Creed. He meticulously explained the standard Protestant theology and doctrine by elaborating what the creed said. Right at the beginning of the first sermon Caron stated that those who longed for true spiritual nourishment should know the most fundamental teaching of Christianity as expressed in the Apostles' Creed, God's Word and the Lord's Prayer. These three foundations, he explained, must be closely observed by all Christians so that they may find a clear mirror that would help them see how to live according to God's will so that they may live as righteous people.

Showing indebtedness to the Portuguese while at the same time also rejecting the teachings of Roman Catholicism, Caron consistently used the term *artigo* for the word "article." He openly stated that this term was originally from Portuguese and he did not hesitate in using the term, because the people were already familiar with it. He explained that the twelve articles were like twelve pillars that work together to support one unity of Christian teaching. He reminded the audience that the number 12 and the name "Apostles' Creed" did not mean that each article was created by the apostles of Jesus, one person for one article, but it was so named because these articles were based on the teaching of the apostles as a whole. Because the word came from the Holy Spirit, he said, Christians could be sure

35. Caron, *Voorbeeldt des openbaeren Godtsdienst*, 170.
36. Caron, *Voorbeeldt des openbaeren Godtsdienst*, 171.

that the written word was truly God's speech. Even though Caron did not use technical terms in explaining the nature of divine special revelation in Scripture, he certainly provided his listeners with a solid belief in the divine nature of the Scripture.

In his exposition of the first article of the creed, Caron delved right away into the doctrine of the Trinity. His elaboration of the creedal statement "I believe in God the Father Almighty" led him into one of the most difficult questions in the Christian faith: how can this one God be three persons? Caron did not try to simplify the doctrine, even to the people whose theological understanding must have still been very elementary. He explained that the Scripture led people to believe that even though God is one, in this one nature of God we have the three persons of Father, Son and Holy Spirit. Caron used the Malay word *parracarra* to simplify his explanation. While the term did not necessary just mean "person" but more had a connotation of things, happenings or existences, he nonetheless used it perhaps to make it easier for his readers to follow his thought. He explained the significance of the personhood of the Trinity later in the sermon. He cited 1 John 5:7 as his scriptural basis for the doctrine. However, he was careful enough not to say that there are "three that bare witness in heaven, the Father, Son and Holy Spirit." He only said that there were three witnesses in heaven, and the three witnesses are actually just one. For him this scriptural text was as close as there could be for a biblical basis for the Trinitarian language.

Caron acknowledged that the truth about the Trinity was something that was deeply hidden in God. As human beings we could only believe quietly. The Malay term he used for believing quietly was *pitsaja diem diem*,[37] perhaps signifying that this doctrine was not supposed to be used as a point of argument or debate with others, especially with the Islamic people because they would not be able to understand the doctrine. In order to provide some analogies for the Trinity, Caron used an Augustinian approach. He was, as he had always been in his sermons, very careful not to put too much load on the hearers. Without mentioning the name of Augustine or the entire Western tradition of the psychological analogy of the Trinity, he stated that in order to understand how the three could be one and the one was in three, people could look into the human soul. There were three distinctly identifiable realities in human soul, namely mind, memory and life force. Even though these were three distinct realities in

---

37. Caron, *Voorbeeldt des openbaeren Godtsdienst*, 6.

The Sermons of Franchois Caron as Further Reinforcement

human life, they were all one as the soul of the individual. He also used the analogy from the sun, stating that light, the rays and heat are three realities that come from the one sun. Just like Augustine he also used fire, flame and heat to give further analogy for the Trinity.[38]

Caron insisted that God is only one. Each divine person is not higher than the other. All three persons are the one true God. Here the readers can see that Caron was careful not to fall into the problem of subordinationism and tritheism all at once. It was necessary for Caron to warn his readers about the danger of either subordinationism or tritheism. The people in Ambon were surrounded by Islamic people as well as followers of tribal religions. Islam denied the reality of the Trinity, thinking that Christianity worshipped three gods. Pagan religions believed in gods that came from other gods, so as to make the new god, sometimes described as the son of another higher-level god, subordinated to the god from whom he derived his being. Caron reminded his readers that the term "God the Father" is used not in the sense that the Father is more superior to the other two members of the Trinity by his nature.

The first reason why the Father is called the Father, Caron explained, is because he is the father of Jesus Christ. Jesus was begotten by the Father, not from a relationship with a woman, but from the very nature of his divinity. Secondly, God the Father is called Father because he has adopted us to be his children. Jesus Christ is the only true Son of God the Father, but in Christ we have been made the children of the heavenly Father. This can only happen because the Holy Spirit has worked in our heart and changed our heart. This doctrinal expression, even though presented in very simple Malay sentences, reflected the deep Calvinistic doctrinal belief of the adoption of the elect to be the children of God. The third reason why God is called the Father is, according to Caron, because God is the Creator of all human beings, together with the rest of the created universe. Because God has created us, we can confidently call God our Father. While the Father is rightly called our Father and our Creator, Caron reminded his audience that they should not forget that the Son and the Holy Spirit are never separated from the Father. At the same time, however, we can distinguish the works of the Trinity in that the Father is the creator, the Son is the redeemer and the Holy Spirit sanctifies us.

God the Father is called the "Father Almighty" because he has the absolute, sovereign power, Caron explained. Human beings, on the other

---

38. Augustine, *De Trinitate*, 8. 14, 9. and 2, 15. 10.

hand, are given some power and authority, but human's authority on the created universe is limited. God is in heaven with his unlimited power, and he never feels tired or finding anything too difficult for him. At this point in the sermon Caron was touching on God's omniscience and omnipotence. To the ordinary Christians in the East Indies Caron did not need to use the technical theological terms. What he needed to tell the people was just the content of the doctrine, presented in avery simple sentence. To the doctrine of divine omnipotence and omniscience Caron added the doctrine of creatio *ex nihilo*. Believing that Moses was the author of Genesis as well as the other four books of the Pentateuch, Caron explicitly said that Moses taught us in Genesis that God created the heavens and the earth without using any pre-existing material. He used examples from daily lives of the Ambonese to illustrate people's occupations and their creative works such as a goldsmith, making jewelry from gold or home builders using stone and wood to make houses. God is not like these artisans, he wrote, because God only needed to speak and everything came into being.

Knowledge of God the Trinity is the true knowledge that will bring people to have eternal life, Caron boldly said in the sermon.[39] This statement reflected well Jesus' teaching in John 17:3, even though he did not cite this passage. At the same time, Caron also seemed to reflect on Calvin's first point in the *Institutes* that all the sum of wisdom and knowledge lies in the knowledge of God and knowledge of self.[40] Caron's insistence on the necessity of the knowledge of the Trinity as the way to eternal life demonstrated how he wanted Christians in the East Indies to have strong knowledge of who God is. As opposed to the Jesuits, who baptized many people in the archipelago and did not seem to be too concerned with the teaching of sufficient knowledge of Scripture, Caron as well as other Dutch ministers in the East Indies worked very hard to provide teaching of Christianity. His sermons are some concrete examples of his insistence that the people must have sufficient knowledge of Scripture.

Staying true to the Reformed understanding of how humans can know God, Caron quickly moved on to the topic of general and special revelation as he preached on the first article of the Apostles' Creed. He stated that we could know God in two ways. The first is by way of looking at God's work in creation, and second by reading God's own word in Scripture. His explanation on how we can know the Creator through his handy work reflected

---

39. Caron, *Voorbeeldt des openbaeren Godtsdienst*, 7.
40. Calvin, *Institutes*, 1.1.1.

the argument from design for the existence of God. He used an example that his listeners would be able to understand well. He said that if one went into a deep jungle and then saw a nice house standing in the middle of the jungle, the person would certainly believe that the house was there because somebody else had built it. The house could not have been in the middle of the jungle accidentally or by chance. In the same manner, he continued, when we look at the entire creation, we are looking at the grandest place for us to dwell. This grand creation could not have happened by chance. God has created this beautiful world, and by looking at this created order we get to know God the Creator.

In the beginning of the second sermon on the Apostles' Creed, Caron reiterated the Reformed view of general and special revelation with more emphasis on special revelation. He stated that even when people can know God the Creator through observing creation, this knowledge would never be sufficient to bring salvation to sinful humanity. Following Calvin's idea of "the seed of religion,"[41] Caron pointed out that even the unbelievers also know a little bit about God and acknowledge God's light and they know that there is God who has magnificent power and is the judge that will charge all humans act and sinfulness, but the unbelievers do not know the true God and cannot enter the kingdom of heaven.[42]

While showing the beauty of God's work in creation and inviting his audience to absorb everything that they could get from the beautiful nature around them, Caron went back to the first chapter of Genesis to show that the text's repeated use of the word "good" to describe God's creation meant that God the Creator is good. The goodness of God, he further pointed out, was shown in the fact that he is willing to create the heavens and the earth even though God does not need anything and he does not lack anything. God's goodness is even more evidence, he said, in creating human beings in his own image, and in making human beings the caretaker of the whole world in order that God's name can be honored all over the world.[43]

Of all the specific families of vegetation that he could use to illustrate the variety of vegetation that God created on the third day, Caron singled out spices as his example. He said that besides creating fruit-bearing trees and grass, God created spices.[44] It is both interesting and ironic that he used

41. Calvin, *Institutes*, 1.3.1.
42. Caron, *Voorbeeldt des openbaeren Godtsdienst*, 9.
43. Caron, *Voorbeeldt des openbaeren Godtsdienst*, 7.
44. Caron, *Voorbeeldt des openbaeren Godtsdienst*, 6.

spices here. Spices were perhaps the most important plants with which the Ambonese had the closest connection. The people were perhaps very proud of the spices that grew in their land, and spices were also among the best examples of God greatness in creation for the people, because of their fragrance and economic, medicinal and preservative values, but spices were also the cause for the Europeans to come to their land and later trample over their freedom and dignity as human beings.

Creation and providence are the two works of God that are never separated. The doctrine of creation and providence was also a significant element in Calvin's theological concept of knowledge of God. Caron stood in line within the Reformed tradition on this topic. As soon as he finished explicating the story of creation as mentioned in Genesis 1, he reminded his listeners that God did not leave his creation to move on its own. He compared God to home builders or ship builders. But, unlike a home builder who built a house and let other people to live in the house, or unlike a ship builder who let another person to be the captain of the ship, God keeps his creation under his care constantly and continuously. Caron beautifully used a feminine imagery to show God's providence. He said that God is like a mother who always takes care and attends to her newborn baby.[45] Caron did not hesitate to use the word *providentia* in this part of the sermon. Perhaps he thought that the people really had to know the term, considering that it was very important in the Reformed tradition, and that there was no Malay word that was good enough to represent the content of the doctrine of divine providence. He explained providence as:

> God's great power over everything, through which power he takes care, attends to, holds, as if with his own hands, the entire heaven and earth and human beings, and everything that has breath. [God's providence] is also over everything that grows from the soil, spices, grass, rain and drought, plentiful harvest or time of famine, [when we] drink and eat, health and sickness, wealthy or poor. These did not happen by chance, but from his will, just as from his own hand.[46]

Caron reminded his readers that this view of divine providence was rooted in the teaching of the Heidelberg Catechism. As it was common in those days, Caron called the Heidelberg Catechism *catechismus besar*, or "the large[er] catechism." The doctrine of providence was indeed an

45. Caron, *Voorbeeldt des openbaeren Godtsdienst*, fol. 6.
46. Caron, *Voorbeeldt des openbaeren Godtsdienst*, 6–7.

important teaching in the Heidelberg Catechism. Questions and answers 26 and 27 of the catechism carefully explain the meaning of God's providence. Caron did not cite the exact reference of the catechism in his sermon, but it is clear from his statement that he had these two questions and answers in mind.

Caron's second sermon on the second article of the Apostles' Creed focuses on Jesus Christ. In this sermon he carefully explained the person and the work of Jesus. The beginning of the sermon took more of the form of a theological lecture than an average Sunday morning sermon. Caron gave his audience a lesson in the significance of knowing the meaning of the name Jesus. He stated that the name came from the Hebrew word for "Savior." Understanding that most of his listeners might have heard the Portuguese talked about Jesus, he said that in Portuguese the term for "Savior" was *Saluwani*, and then he also provided the Malay word *Juretouboussan* as the equivalent of "Savior." This reference to multiple languages showed how Caron was sensitive to his audience's situation. He then continued by saying that the Malay term *Juretoubousan* when applied to Jesus meant that he is the only one who can release human beings from danger and provide safety.[47]

In making the significance of the meaning of Jesus' name even more deeply embedded in his audience's minds, Caron compared the process of naming newborn babies at baptism and how Jesus received his name. He indicated that at church babies were named as they were baptized, and the name was usually chosen either by the parents of the baby or by the witnesses. Jesus, on the other hand, was given this name by the very reason of who he is as Savior. This name was told to Joseph by the angel as mentioned in Matthew 1. This short statement is very valuable for us today, because it gives us a good look at how the naming of the baby took place at baptism in the East Indies. We can see that the liturgy of baptism in the Reformed church in the East Indies followed the European liturgy in which the name was given at baptism and not before.

As Paul wrote in Romans 5, because of Adam's sin all people, who are the descendants of Adam, have fallen into sin. Caron explained that human's sinfulness in Adam meant that all humans were indebted to God, because of their rebellion and trespasses against God. Humans could not pay their own debt, and only Jesus Christ could pay their debt and covered human's sin so that we could appear righteous in front of God. Caron

---

47. Caron, *Voorbeeldt des openbaeren Godtsdienst*, 9.

further said that the death of Christ on the cross appeased God's wrath because Christ was willing to take up humans' sins on his own shoulder. The death of Christ also functioned as the antidote for our death, so that we did not have to be punished in hell, but we could enter heaven. This part of the sermon shows us how Caron touched on the view of atonement. He clearly believed in the Reformed view of the imputation of Christ's righteousness on sinful humanity. And even if he did not cite former theologians who had elaborated their views on atonement, we can see that Caron believed in the death of Christ as the satisfaction for God's wrath in that Christ appeased God's anger and therefore enabled humans to receive forgiveness.

Caron openly criticized the Roman Catholics for praying to saints, or to angels, or to statues. He emphasized that sinful human beings could only be saved by Jesus because there is no other name under heaven through which we could be saved. And in order to create a dramatic contrast in the sermon, he invited his readers to sing together with the Virgin Mary, to let their soul magnify the Lord and their spirit rejoices in God who is Savior.[48] This explicit mention of Virgin Mary was a clear display that Caron wanted to be deeply biblical in showing that salvation only came from God through Jesus, and that the Roman Catholics were wrong in praying to Mary as one of the most important saints in their lives.

Caron's lesson on the person and works of Christ continued with an explanation that the name "Christ" in Greek meant "the Anointed One." He showed that in the Old Testament three offices required anointing, namely king, priest and prophet. He interchanged the Arabic words *califa* and *imam* to refer to "priest,"[49] giving us the impression that at that time the words were already widely used by the people in the East Indies, and that he was not hesitated in using these Arabic terms because it helped him communicate his message to the audience. Just as the anointing on these three offices meant that the people holding the offices were given authority, Jesus also holds the authority in himself. The only difference between Jesus and the Old Testament was that in Jesus the three offices were merged in his own personhood. Caron went on in explaining the significance of kingship, priesthood and prophetic role in Jesus Christ. From there Caron gave his listeners some practical application on what it meant for Christians to have Jesus as king, priest and prophet. Caron used the imagery of oil as it was poured on a person's head would flow to the person's entire body, so it was

---

48. Caron, *Voorbeeldt des openbaeren Godtsdienst*, 10.
49. Caron, *Voorbeeldt des openbaeren Godtsdienst*, 10.

also true that the oil of Christ would flow to his people, so that the people could also become kings, priests and prophets. As prophets Christians had the ability to become witnesses of the truth of God's word and to tell other people that Christianity was the only true religion. The priestly role of Christians could be expressed through their lives that were completely dedicated to God, worshipping God constantly and be merciful and kind to other people, so that Christ would be represented by the kindness and good deeds of his people. Without citing Paul in Romans 12:1-2, Caron showed that Christians fulfilled the priestly office by way of making themselves living sacrifice to God. As kings Christians were called to lead their own lives and also others in the fight against the powers of the devil.

Just as what he did to the Roman Catholics, Caron was also not shy in criticizing Islam. He pointed out that the Koran had misunderstood the reality of Jesus as the Son of God.[50] Jesus is called the Son of God he said, not because of his humanity, but because of his divinity. The term "son" was used to refer to Jesus because he has the same essence as God the Father, just like a human son has the same human nature as his father. Caron directly delved into the discussion of the equality, eternity and unity of the divine nature of the Father and the Son. Unlike human fathers who must exist before their sons are born, God the Father did not exist before God the Son, he explained. The Father and the Son have always existed in all eternity. The Father and the Son are not two separate individuals like a human father and his son, but they are one God in two distinct persons. Caron used the Malay term *saxi* to refer to the persons of the Godhead. The use of the term *saxi* is interesting, because it actually means "witness." This was a good choice of word to translate the term "person" into Malay. As witnesses testify about something, Caron seemed to want to show that the three persons of the Godhead are witnesses to the entire divine nature who is God the Trinity. In the long talk about the divine nature of Christ in this sermon, Caron in essence gave his audience a summary of the meaning of *homoousios* of the Council of Nicea without naming the first ecumenical council in the history of Christianity.

A sermon about the person and works of Jesus should never leave out the Chalcedonian definition of the two natures of Christ. Without ever mentioning the name "Council of Chalcedon" he told the people that Jesus is both truly human and truly divine. Jesus had his humanity from the Virgin Mary and his divinity from God the Father. The two natures are always

---

50. Caron, *Voorbeeldt des openbaeren Godtsdienst*, 12.

together in Jesus, never separated and never confused. As the true God, Jesus created the heavens and the earth and holds the world in his hands, and also, when he was on earth, he healed people and even raised Lazarus from the dead. We worship Jesus who is God the same way we worship God the Father, Caron further reminded his readers. And then, following Anselm's argument in his *Cur Deus Homo?*, Caron explained that only as true God could Jesus redeem fallen humanity. If Jesus had not been the true God, he could not have been able to redeem all people who had fallen into sin, and he could not have been raised from the dead and defeated Satan. Jesus was also truly human because it was humanity that fell into sin and therefore a true human being must die for humans' sins.

The belief in the virgin birth of Jesus was an important topic that Caron did not want to miss in teaching the basic beliefs of Christianity. He realized that this topic was difficult for the Christians in the East Indies to grasp, and even more difficult for them to talk about it with other people outside of the church. The Islamic people in the island rejected this belief as plain blasphemy, and the pagans simply laughed at such a concept. But in his sermon on the third article of the creed Caron took the time to explain the virgin birth, because it was the center of Christians' understanding of the two natures of Jesus. He had discussed the divinity of Jesus in the preceding sermon, and in this sermon he stated that Jesus was truly human because he received the human nature from Mary his mother. Jesus must become fully and truly human because he had to save fallen humanity from sin. Repeating the Anselmian view of the significance of the incarnation, he reminded his hearers that Jesus must be the substitute for human sin and this was all possible because of God's great love to human beings. God had given his only beloved Son to be the Savior because God so loved the world, and he was willing to redeem the world through Jesus Christ. Caron reminded his readers that in the redemptive work of Jesus the three persons of the Trinity are never separated from each other. He said that even though Jesus was incarnated and took our human nature, and God the Father and the Holy Spirit were always with Jesus in his incarnated state, the Trinity was never changed. He emphasized that the Father and the Holy Spirit never became human, only the Son took our human nature and lived among us.[51]

In his theological explanation about the two natures of Christ, Caron stayed faithful to the Chalcedonian statement of the doctrine without

---

51. Caron, *Voorbeeldt des openbaeren Godtsdienst*, 14.

unnecessarily burdening his readers with a lecture on the history of the doctrine. He only mentioned—very briefly—that a long time ago several ministers had wrestled with the question of the two nature of Christ, and came up with the explanation to help Christians to know well and to prevent them from falling into false teaching.[52] He simply said in the sermon that Jesus is always the eternal God together with the Father and the Holy Spirit, but in the one person Jesus the divine nature was never mixed with the human nature, even when Jesus took up the human nature. The divine nature was never reduced, but always coexisting with the human nature.[53]

Jesus' true humanity should be embraced as biblical truth. Caron listed several points of biblical evidence that Jesus was truly human, including the fact that Jesus was hungry and thirsty, that when he was in a location he could not be in a different place, and that he dwelled among his disciples and the disciples saw his physical reality. Caron also cited some biblical stories that show Jesus' emotion, including his anger and sadness. Jesus' death and the reality that his body was buried became another proof for Caron to show that Jesus was fully human. And when Jesus rose again from the dead, Thomas' request was a proof that the resurrected Jesus was also the same Jesus who was crucified on the cross.

Caron did not leave out the opportunity to tell his listeners that even though Jesus was truly and fully human, he was also sinless. The fact that he was born of Virgin Mary did not make Jesus inherit the sinfulness that Mary—and the rest of the human race—carried. Jesus was conceived by the Holy Spirit, and this is the very reason why Jesus did not inherit the sinfulness of human nature. Caron openly attacked the teaching of the Roman Catholic Church that said that Mary too was born sinless. He insisted that out of the sinful nature that Mary had, Jesus was born holy and sinless just as God is holy and sinless. He insisted that the work of the Holy Spirit in the birth of Jesus was so special, that inside Mary's womb the Holy Spirit had worked so that the divine and human natures could exist together in Jesus in the blink of an eye.[54]

Caron ended the sermon with a practical application and a call for the people to worship God and to love him constantly, because God had given us the greatest gift of salvation in Christ. In Jesus God had demonstrated the greatest love, therefore it was fitting for the people to reciprocate and

---

52. Caron, *Voorbeeldt des openbaeren Godtsdienst*, 16.
53. Caron, *Voorbeeldt des openbaeren Godtsdienst*, 14.
54. Caron, *Voorbeeldt des openbaeren Godtsdienst*, 16.

love him too. He reminded the people that they should not follow the devil or take the sinful way of life. but to follow God, who is holy, because God has washed, loved and made them righteous and holy. In the sermon Caron demonstrated theological leanings toward the view of limited atonement. While he did not push too hard on this theological issue, he stated in his fourth sermon on the creed that the blood of Jesus that was poured on the cross was not typical human blood. He wrote in the sermon that it was "the blood of God, through which he has redeemed *Christians*."[55] Caron's deliberate use of "the blood of God" indicated that he considered this doctrine to be very important. All throughout his sermons he strongly maintained that God is spirit, and therefore people should not think of God as a physical being. But here he explicitly said that the blood of Jesus was the blood of God. He made this statement within the context of the Anselmian thought that because Jesus was the true God his death was worth much more than anything people could imagine. In emphasizing the unlimited value of the blood of Jesus Caron was willing to make such a shocking claim that the blood was God's blood, seemingly contradicting his consistent emphasis of the spiritual nature of God. This blood, he further mentioned, was for the redemption for Christians. Here is where we see Caron's leaning toward limited atonement. He used the term *himponan Nassarani* to refer to God's people. The Malay-speaking people in the East Indies knew that the term meant Christians. Caron did not use the term "elect" to show the recipients of Christ's redeeming blood, but for his listeners the term *Nassarani* was enough to show that the blood of Jesus was not meant for everyone. The blood—and thus the atoning work of Christ—was only for Christians, namely people who believe in Christ. Furthermore, the Malay word *himponan* signified the idea of a group of people that is different from another group. When we read this in the context of the efficacy of Christ's blood we can confidently say that Caron meant that the blood of Jesus was only for a select group of people, the true children of God.

The Calvinists in the East Indies were indebted to the Portuguese for their vocabulary. Caron interchanged between the terms *cajo krus* and *cajo riggang* to refer to the cross of Jesus. It is obvious that the term *krus* came from Portuguese. *Riggang* was a Malay term for a cross-like structure. The Malay term *cajo* or *cajou* simply means "wood." In the earlier decades of the seventeenth century, as was evidenced from the translations of the Heidelberg Catechism and *De Wegh na den Hemel*, the Portuguese-influenced

---

55. Caron, *Voorbeeldt des openbaeren Godtsdienst*, 19.

The Sermons of Franchois Caron as Further Reinforcement

word *krus* was more preferred, possibly because the Portuguese had used the term extensively. However, toward the latter part of the seventeenth century, as Caron was making this collection of sermons available to the people, there seemed to be a development in which Christians in the East Indies started to use the term *riggang* for the cross. Therefore, in this collection of sermons Caron interchanged between the two terms, so that the people could move more toward the use of the Malay word *riggang* instead of the Portuguese—and thus Catholic—use of *krus*.

The doctrine of the state of humiliation of Christ took center stage in Caron's sermon. Caron painted a good and clear picture of how Christ was humiliated since birth, by being born in a manger. He took the seventeenth-century daily life of the rural people in the East Indies as his way to make his point. He said that the baby Jesus must sleep in the grass. He did not mention hay since in the East Indies cattle did not normally eat hay. Grass was always found in abundance in that part of the world, and thus it made better sense when Caron contextualized his sermon in this way. Caron summarized the life and ministry of Jesus easily for his hearers, and he further contextualized it when he talked about the payment that Judas received for betraying Jesus. Instead of using the biblical expression "thirty pieces of silver" Caron used "fifteen Real" as the payment for Jesus. Real was the name of the currency commonly used by the people in the East Indies at that time. From Caron's statement we could deduct that one Real was worth two pieces of silver coin, and thus Caron used fifteen Real for Judas' payment.

Caron went into the detail of the passion of Christ in showing that the humiliation and agony that Christ went through was for the salvation of his people. He took the time to explain how the Roman system of crucifixion was the most horrible form of execution. In describing Christ's condition in being hung on the cross he stated that the body of Christ was so stretched on the cross just like when the Ambonese stretched a piece of skin on the traditional drum that the people usually made for their musical performances, called the *tifa*.[56] The Ambonese really knew how much a piece of skin must be stretched in order to fit onto the frame of a *tifa* to make the drum sound well. This illustration helped the people to visualize how Jesus suffered on the cross.

The substitution that Jesus did on our behalf was a belief that Caron wanted to instill in the minds of his readers. He made a point in showing

---

56. Caron, *Voorbeeldt des openbaeren Godtsdienst*, 20.

that because Christ took our place by taking the curse and punishment of sin in his death on the cross, we are now guaranteed the eternal life. This concept of substitution, he said, was already prefigured in the Old Testament. God replaced Isaac with a ram so that Abraham did not have to sacrifice his son. At the same time, Caron also alluded to the Old Testament passage that said that whoever died hung on a tree was cursed by God, and showed that Jesus took up the curse of our sin so that we can be made right with God. In this statement he criticized the Islamic teaching that said that the person crucified was not Jesus but one of his disciples, or even Simon the Cyrene. Caron argued that if Jesus was not the one who underwent the crucifixion, then our sins could not have been pardoned by God. He insisted that Jesus must be the one to replace us to pay for our sinfulness.

Caron also reminded his readers that even though Jesus died, it was not the divine nature of Jesus that died. The divinity of Jesus would never die. Without elaborating on the issue of body and soul in the one personhood of Jesus, Caron said that when Jesus died, his soul has left his body, and it was clear through the word of Jesus on the cross when he left his soul into the Father's hand. He showed that the death of Jesus was similar to the death of human beings in that the soul was separated from the body. In this statement we see how Caron emphasized once again the true humanity of Jesus.

The death of Jesus was the fulfillment of God's curse on Adam and Eve. When God forbade our first parents from eating the fruit of the knowledge of good and evil, God said that Adam and Eve would die if they ate the fruit. The death of the human Jesus, Caron believed, was to bring the curse of God upon Adam and Eve to completion. With the death of Jesus God's wrath has now been appeased, and the result is that we can have eternal life. Caron's elaborate and detailed sermon on the significance of the death of Jesus for human salvation is a good example of his effort to bring the good news of the gospel to the people. Caron demonstrated eagerness to ensure that the people really understand what being followers of Jesus meant. It meant eternal salvation, and this should be the most important desire for all people. Thus, even though he did not come to the East Indies as a missionary in the traditional sense of the word, Caron actually did the work of a missionary. He wanted to ensure that his audience knew why believing in Jesus Christ as the only Savior mattered to them. It was the only way that the people could be saved.

The Sermons of Franchois Caron as Further Reinforcement

The contrast between Christian faith and other religions cannot be wider than the belief in the resurrected Savior. Other religions may have similar emphasis on morality and conduct to what is taught in Christianity, but other religions do not believe in the founder of their religion who died and rose again. Caron made sure that Christians who read or heard his sermon understood this very fundamental belief of Christianity. In the fifth sermon on the Apostles' Creed he referred back to several Gospel stories about the resurrection of Jesus. He pointed out that the testimony of several eyewitnesses of the resurrected Jesus could not be wrong. The Gospel writers believed that Jesus was alive.[57] His strong belief in the resurrected Jesus was contrasted with what some Islamic people had been told, namely that Mohammad promised the Arabic that he would be resurrected too. But Caron showed that it was almost a thousand years since Muhammad had died and there had been no sign that Muhammad would be coming back.[58] As the readers could expect, Caron did not provide a reference for his statement about Muhammad. He must have heard this story circulated among the Muslims and he just used it to make the contrast between Christianity and Islam even sharper.

The resurrection of Christ means that God's children will also be resurrected the same way as Jesus had been resurrected. Caron strongly believed that God's children do not have to go through any punishment because their sins have been forgiven and Jesus has replaced their punishment. What is left is that believers can live as free and forgiven people. He used the Calvinist imagery of grafting when he showed that believers have been united with Christ just like a new branch has been grafted into the stem of a tree. In the process of grafting the new branch nurses out of the main stem and thus it is one with the stem. This imagery must have been easily understood by the people in the East Indies since they lived mostly as farmers. These farmers knew very well how to graft and this knowledge helped Caron in communicating the Calvinist view of union with Christ.[59]

Like Calvin, Caron often used the imagery of a mirror to show that Jesus reflects to his people all the richness and greatness of God.[60] Caron stated that we can look at the resurrection of Jesus as our mirror to see that we will experience something similar. The resurrection of Jesus was

---

57. Caron, *Voorbeeldt des openbaeren Godtsdienst*, 25.
58. Caron, *Voorbeeldt des openbaeren Godtsdienst*, 26.
59. Caron, *Voorbeeldt des openbaeren Godtsdienst*, 27.
60. Calvin, *Institutes*, 3.24.5.

The Way to Heaven

a bodily resurrection that we can look forward to. This resurrection can strengthen the faith of the believers, because we will live forever with Christ. Because Jesus is our head, Caron said, we as the body of Christ will also live again. The head will never be separated from the body, and therefore whatever happened to the head will also happen to the body. In this part of the sermon Caron strongly demonstrated the Reformed view of the end time. Instead of being a horrifying time, the end time will be the most glorious event for believers. Caron clearly showed that this belief is a comfort for all believers. He said that we should not fear death, because even in death we will never be separated from Jesus. Without mentioning the Heidelberg Catechism he stated that we all belong, body and soul, in life and in death, to our Savior Jesus Christ.[61]

The state of humiliation that Christ underwent was not separated from the state of exaltation. The resurrection of Jesus was the most wonderful evidence of Christ's exaltation. Caron pointed out this Reformed belief beautifully as he painted the picture of the ascension of Christ in his sixth sermon on the Creed. Caron contrasted the humbleness of Christ's birth which started his state of humiliation with the glory of the ascension which signified his exaltation. Caron reminded his readers that the ascended Jesus was the same human Jesus who came into the world, died, was buried but then lived again. There was still the continuity of the human nature of Jesus, but after the resurrection there was discontinuity as well. The resurrected body of Jesus did not have similar a property as the pre-crucified Jesus. After the resurrection the body could become weightless, so that Jesus could depart from the earth even without wings. Caron attributed this new property to the divine nature of Jesus. The exaltation of Jesus, according to Caron, was also demonstrated by the fact that the cloud covered him completely. Caron made a distinction between heaven and the sky. He mentioned that even though Jesus left the earth and went up into the sky and then the clouds covered him, Jesus did not reside in the sky. He went back to heaven to where the Father is. Heaven, Caron believed, is also the place where the angels are, and the place where the souls of believers who already died reside. In this brief statement we can see that Caron showed the standard teaching of the Reformed faith. The doctrine of the intermediate state seemed to be the underlying thought that Calvin expressed in this sermon. This statement clearly meant that Caron did not belief in the sleep of the soul, but in the active, conscious state of the souls of believers when

---

61. Caron, *Voorbeeldt des openbaeren Godtsdienst*, 28.

they die and wait for the second coming of Christ. Quoting John 14, he emphasized that heaven is the place that Jesus called his Father's house.[62]

The Gospel stories recorded that the ascension of Jesus took place on the Mount of Olives. Caron seemed to show some creative work in translating the name of the mountain. Olives were foreign to the people in the East Indies. Instead of plainly use the word for "olives," which would not mean much to his listeners, Caron provided a free translation that also included some interpretive element to the process, calling the place "the hill of the fruit that produces oil," or *bukit boa minjak* in Malay.[63] This free translation resulted in a somewhat clumsy phrase. The word *boa* in Malay means "fruit" and *minjak* means "oil." This translation demonstrated Caron's sensitivity to his audience. Since his audience had never seen olives he altogether avoided the use of the word "olives" and was satisfied with translating olives into a fruit that was mainly used to produce oil.

The reality that the body of Jesus ascended to heaven, for Caron, meant that Jesus' human body is no longer on earth. He emphasized this to reject the Roman Catholic doctrine of transubstantiation. He openly attacked the doctrine of transubstantiation by saying that it was wrong to believe that the body of Jesus was still present in the bread and wine, even when the Roman Catholic Church taught that Jesus' promise in Mathew 28 that Jesus said he would always be with the disciples to the end of the time should be interpreted as the textual foundation for the physical presence of Jesus in the Eucharist.[64] The belief that God is spirit should not be used as the grounds to think that it is possible for the body of Jesus to be present in the bread and wine, either. The promise that Jesus will always be with us, Caron insisted, did not give the warrant to believe in transubstantiation, because Jesus is present among his people through the Holy Spirit, through his word, by giving us comfort and by giving us the heavenly blessing in which we feel the presence of Jesus. Moreover, he pointed out that the church, the community of believers, was the avenue through which Jesus would be present among the people.

Christ is now exalted at the right hand of God the Father. Caron told his people that the expression "sitting on the right hand of God the Father" should not be understood literally, because God is spirit and God the Father does not have physical hands. This metaphor should be understood

---

62. Caron, *Voorbeeldt des openbaeren Godtsdienst*, 29.
63. Caron, *Voorbeeldt des openbaeren Godtsdienst*, 30.
64. Caron, *Voorbeeldt des openbaeren Godtsdienst*, 31.

The Way to Heaven

as the most important and honored place that one could think of. Caron reminded the people that worldly kings were used to placing their most important advisors to sit on their right hand side. The creedal expression, therefore, means that Jesus has the most honored and exalted place. However, even though this expression is metaphorical, Caron also said that it is not without biblical grounds. Jesus himself told Caiaphas that he would see the Son of Man sitting on the right hand of God. In addition, Paul also mentioned in one of his letters that Jesus is seated on the right hand of God to pray on our behalf.[65]

The second coming of Christ should be understood well by all believers. Caron was clear on his intention to show the separation between God's elect and the reprobates. He used the passage in Matthew where Jesus talked about the separation between the sheep and the goats as his biblical text. He was firm in showing that the second coming of Christ will bring judgment for the reprobates, but ultimate glory for the elect. The judgment will include condemnation of Satan and the fallen angels. He elaborated his belief about the second coming of Christ and the final judgment in the seventh sermon on the Apostles' Creed.[66] He also reminded his audience that the second coming of Christ will be visible and audible, with the voice of the trumpet. The dead will be raised from the grave. Repeating what Paul wrote in 1 Thessalonians, Caron told his listeners that the second coming of Christ will happen soon, but nobody knows when it will happen. What is important for believers, he said, is to be prepared. He strongly demonstrated that the second coming of Christ is integrated in the great plan of God for his creation. God created the heavens and the earth, and God will also bring the present age into its ending, but with continuity into the new reality in the second coming of Christ.[67]

Caron showed that just as the Bible had said, the signs of the second coming were clearly visible to the people: war, famine and natural disasters. He also alluded to Paul's statement that people had become selfish, arrogant, blasphemous and hypocritical. Then he called the pope the final and last example of all the evil characteristics of human beings in the final days of this present age. This critique of the pope was very strong and it was reflective of what the Reformed church thought regarding the pope. Caron called the pope "Papa Romano" and he charged the pope as the one

65. Caron, *Voorbeeldt des openbaeren Godtsdienst*, 32.
66. Caron, *Voorbeeldt des openbaeren Godtsdienst*, 36.
67. Caron, *Voorbeeldt des openbaeren Godtsdienst*, 37.

who "elevated himself as the head of all Christians." He explicitly said that in the end God will throw away the pope.[68] This thought clearly expressed Caron's stance—and the company of the Reformed ministers from the Netherlands—regarding the papacy. This thought was an overflow of the Reformation time, and in the middle of the seventeenth century the sentiment was transported to the East Indies. In Ambon and other islands where Roman Catholicism had had some presence prior to the arrival of the Dutch, the people must have been taught by the Jesuits to regard the pope as the highest leader of the church. However, the Reformed ministers from the Netherlands must have felt compelled to fight this teaching. Therefore, in this sermon regarding the second coming of Christ Caron used his opportunity to show the people the standpoint of the Reformed church.

Caron understood the difficulty that the people of the East Indies had in understanding the Holy Spirit. He explained in the eighth sermon on the creed that the word for "spirit" can be interpreted as "wind, or "human breath" or "disembodied being."[69] He explained that the Portuguese used the word *spirito* to refer to the spirit. This explanation shows that Caron was making a connection with the translations of the catechisms as discussed earlier in this book. The earlier translations of the catechisms still adopted the Portuguese term *spirito* because it would make the indigenous people understand who the Holy Spirit is, considering that the Jesuits used the word extensively. Caron also mentioned that in Malay the word for "spirit" was *arouah*, the reality of our being that resides in the human body, and therefore invisible to human eyes. He also told the people that angels were spirits. Despite his repeated emphasis that spirits are disembodied beings, Caron had to use some type of physical analogy to explain the procession of the Holy Spirit from the Father. He said that the Holy Spirit comes out of the Father in a similar fashion as human breath comes out of the nostrils or mouth. He referred to the risen Jesus when he met the disciples in the locked room and blew his breath onto the disciples as his biblical grounds for his explanation of the procession of the Holy Spirit. The Holy Spirit is called "holy" because he is the one sanctifying his people, making them holy and righteous. Caron then briefly made a comment that may be an indication of his stand on the issue of irresistible grace. He said that the Holy Spirit will make his people holy and righteous, by way of washing away their sins and changing their hearts any time and anywhere the Holy Spirit

68. Caron, *Voorbeeldt des openbaeren Godtsdienst*, 38.
69. Caron, *Voorbeeldt des openbaeren Godtsdienst*, 39.

wills, and nobody can prevent the Holy Spirit from doing what he does in the hearts of people.[70] Even though Caron did not make too much elaboration of what he meant, this statement may be seen as a good indication of his belief that whenever the Holy Spirit comes to a person and applies the work of Christ's redemption in the heart of that person, there is no way that the person can resist the work of the Holy Spirit.

Caron delved into the doctrine of the Trinity deeper in his expansion of the creedal statement on the Holy Spirit. He further explained the meaning of personhood for the Father, Son and Holy Spirit. In his former sermons he used the Malay term *saxi*, meaning "witness," to refer to the three persons. In this sermon he went further by calling each member of the Trinity *persona*.[71] He explained that each person of the Trinity shares the same substance or nature of the Godhead, but each is distinct as individual witness to the Godhead. The distinctness of the Holy Spirit was seen in the Gospel story of the baptism of Jesus, when the Holy Spirit descended as a dove and the Father spoke to the Son. Caron was against the view that the Holy Spirit does not have an essence but only some sort of influence or power that comes from God. He then reminded his readers that there were not three gods. The three persons are not separated from each other. He also reminded the people not to fall into the mistake of modalism. Even though, as he always did in his sermons, Caron did not use the technical term, he told the people that it would be wrong to consider the Trinity as one person who took different roles, one occasion as the Father, another as the Son and at another occasion as the Holy Spirit. He took Jesus' words in John 14:6 as his foundation to show that each person of the Trinity is distinct from the others. Jesus said that he would ask the Father to send another comforter. This must mean, Caron said, that the three persons are distinguishable from each other. Otherwise, the words of Jesus would not make any sense. Caron then provided the standard, orthodox description of the distinctiveness of each person, in that The Father is the only unbegotten one who begat the Son from all eternity, the Son is the only begotten one from the Father, and the Holy Spirit proceeds from both the Father and the Son and receives substance from both the Father and the Son.[72] Caron's explanation of the doctrine of the Trinity reflected the characteristic of Western Christianity in his emphasis that the Holy Spirit proceeds from both the Father and the

---

70. Caron, *Voorbeeldt des openbaeren Godtsdienst*, 39.
71. Caron, *Voorbeeldt des openbaeren Godtsdienst*, 40.
72. Caron, *Voorbeeldt des openbaeren Godtsdienst*, 40.

The Sermons of Franchois Caron as Further Reinforcement

Son, unlike the position held by the Eastern Church, which believes that the Holy Spirit proceeds only from the Father. This short explanation on the Trinity is remarkable in that Caron was willing to talk about it in his sermon for the people in the East Indies to understand. This is another example in which he showed how he saw the importance of teaching doctrine to the people without simplifying the doctrine. Caron must have realized that the doctrine of the Trinity was the most abstract and difficult to grasp. However, given the challenges that Christians in the East Indies had to face constantly from the Islamic people surrounding them, it was of the utmost necessity that Caron teach them this doctrine.

Caron took the time to argue that the Bible affirmed the divinity of the Holy Spirit. He used stories and teachings from the Old and New Testaments that demonstrate the Holy Spirit as having the same divine nature and character as God. The Holy Spirit is omnipresent, omniscient and omnipotent in the same way the Bible describes God. In the Old Testament the Holy Spirit worked in God's people to give them skills to build the tabernacle or to speak as prophets to represent God to the people.

As a Reformed minister, Caron pointed out that the very first work in the heart of people is to convict people of their sins and to bring them to repent. Then the Holy Spirit illumines the minds of the people so that they can understand the word of God and can have a saving relationship with God through Jesus Christ. Thus, the Holy Spirit turns the heart that was darkened by sin into a clean heart that is humble and obedient to God.[73] Caron used feminine imagery to explain how the Holy Spirit takes care of God's people. He said that the Spirit is like a mother who carefully raises her child so that thet will be nourished and live well. He connected this work of the Holy Spirit with the sacraments; first baptism gives people new life, like the birth of a baby, and then the Lord's Supper provides food for the children of God. Furthermore, the Holy Spirit keeps holding God's children like a mother teaching her child to walk straight, and when the children fall she raises them up again. As an application of his sermon Caron reminded the people that even when they sin the Holy Spirit will always help them return to God because the Holy Spirit is like our mother. This feminine metaphor for the Holy Spirit was striking and at the same time comforting. Even in the patriarchal society of the people in the East Indies, Caron was willing to highlight the role of a mother as his metaphor. It gave comfort to the people who heard this sermon, because then they could see that God

---

73. Caron, *Voorbeeldt des openbaeren Godtsdienst*, 41.

the Holy Spirit is not like a distant God or impersonal power of God, but as the third member of the Trinity the Holy Spirit will always be close to the people and will lead and guide the people, even when they fail to obey God.

In line with his Reformed conviction, Caron emphasized that the Holy Spirit first comes into the heart of an individual and stirs their heart to repent from all sin before the person can ever do any good works. The very first sign that the Spirit is in the heart of the person, Caron said, is the reality in which the person feels the weight of sins that brings her to hear God's calling for repentance, and then she invites the Holy Spirit to live in her heart. The Holy Spirit who convicts the person of all sins and leads her to repentant will always dwell in her forever. The closing paragraph of his eighth sermon on the Apostles' Creed is a strong demonstration of how Caron adhered to the Reformed view of the Holy Spirit. However, it is also important to see that in the same sermon Caron emphasized the need for individual believers to hold on to the Holy Spirit and keep their own heart clean and free from all sin. He repeatedly called the people to be very careful with the way they lived, avoiding any sinful acts and upholding the high standard of Christian living. On a first glance, Caron's repeated exhortations for the people to live holy might sound contrary to the Reformed belief that salvation does not depend on what we do but is thoroughly by God's grace. One might misunderstand Caron by thinking that he thought that there was no perseverance of the saints. However, a closer look at Caron's intention will reveal that he did not intend to preach on salvation by works, nor did he worry that the people would lose their salvation if they did not keep their lives holy. These exhortations actually served as Caron's expression of the practice of the Reformed churches in Europe in their insistence that Christians must live morally. In Calvin's Geneva the consistory functioned as a policing body to ensure that Christians lived according to a high moral standard. While the practice of summoning people to come before the consistory for violations of various ecclesial rules was not applied in the East Indies, Caron's exhortations may be seen as a midway between the extreme consistory-controlled behavior and complete liberty of people's way of life. For the people in the East Indies, there should be a visible manifestation of their religious lives, and Caron saw the need to remind the people how to be living witnesses of their faith.

The community of believers was visibly expressed through the church. But believers are also members of the universal, invisible church. Caron explained the difference between the visible and invisible church in his ninth sermon on the Creed. He explained that church could mean a local church such as in Ambon, Banda or Batavia. But church could also mean all God's children, the true believers, who were God's elect and had been granted eternal life. He explicitly stated that the ninth article of the creed included both the visible and the invisible church. In his sermon Caron simply borrowed the Portuguese word *igresia*[74] to refer to the church. It is important to note here that Caron and also other Dutch ministers in the East Indies did not insist on using Dutch words for religious terms. He simply adopted the Portuguese words that the Ambonese had been familiar with. Thus, it shows that Caron and the other ministers were willing to accept what the Portuguese left behind as long as it would make the people understand the concept better.

In agreement with the standard Reformed view of the church, Caron stated that there were four marks of the church, namely one, holy, catholic and apostolic. He took the time in explaining in great detail all these four marks. He saw the oneness or the unity of the church primarily through the fact that the church is the body of Christ. He returned to his understanding of the universal church to explain the unity of the church. He told his audience that the unity of the church is secured by the fact that we all have one father, God, and one mother, the church. Caron demonstrated that he was a strong follower of the Reformed church in seeing the church as mother. This conviction, stemming from the early church's time, most notably in the writings of Cyprian, had been the strongly held position of the medieval church, through the Reformation and into the era of Protestant orthodoxy. While the Roman Catholic Church also emphasized the motherhood of the church as the guarantee of the unity of all the Catholics all over the world, the Reformed Protestants held similar position. Caron did not elaborate the meaning of the church as a mother, because for him it was enough to tell the people that the motherhood of the church and the fatherhood of God are the two main foundations for the unity of the church. This familial imagery brought him to continue his thought by saying that we have one Lord, Jesus Christ, one baptism, one Communion and one confession. In closing his thought regarding the unity of the church Caron used an interesting metaphor that was not commonly used in the Reformed circle in Europe. He said that the unity of the church is expressed through the fact that Christians have one shepherd and all the sheep are in one stable. This metaphor reflected some biblical passages that reminded

---

74. Caron, *Voorbeeldt des openbaeren Godtsdienst*, 45 and passim.

the people of Jesus as the Good Shepherd. And perhaps Caron also thought about Jesus' statement about Judgment Day in Matthew 25, where the goats are separated from the sheep. And for the people in the rural areas in the East Indies, the metaphor worked well. Each farmer had his own stable with his own sheep gathered in one stable. All the sheep belonged to the one farmer, who was usually also the shepherd of the sheep. Therefore, the sheep would see their shepherd as their only leader and owner. The idea of belonging as one flock became a clear image for the people to see that they were all one as the people of God.

The holiness of the church was understood by way of the reality that the church, the community of believers, had been separated from the rest of the world and from the followers of Satan.[75] Caron simply followed the biblical idea that holiness means separation or being set aside. In his sermons Caron consistently used the Malay word *sakti* for "holy" or "holiness." The employment of the word *sakti* indicates that Caron saw the people who were sanctified by the Holy Spirit somehow owned a special gift, a power to be special and to be other than the rest of the community. This specialness was expressed through his comparison between true believers and people of other religions. Caron said that even though in all cities and villages there were Muslims, pagans and people from various religious convictions, these people were not the same as the believers. God dwells or resides in the lives of the believers, God sanctifies them through the blood of his Son and changes the heart of each believer through the work of the Holy Spirit. Therefore, Caron believed that being *sakti* is not the result of the believers' own work, but solely the work of God.

The catholicity of the church lies in the fact that Christianity is the only true religion. In explaining the catholicity of the church Caron had the universal or invisible church in mind. He stated that the true church is the community of all God's people from the beginning of the universe until the end. The people became God's people because of the preaching of the word of God and through the work of the Holy Spirit who made the people to be God's people. Caron did not spend too much time in explaining the catholicity of the church. In his sermon he used the Malay term *mousina* for "universal." Caron did not use the term for "catholic," perhaps because the term was not introduced to the people at that time.

Caron provided a brief history of the origin of the name "Christian." He explained that the disciples of Jesus spread the gospel among the pagans

---

75. Caron, *Voorbeeldt des openbaeren Godtsdienst*, 45.

and the followers of Jesus were called "Christian" for the first time in the city of Antioch. Today, Caron continued, the believers were called Christians because, just as a wife takes the last name of her husband, the church takes Christ's name as her identity. Caron pointed out that when a wife takes her husband's last name the wife belongs to her husband. Here again, Caron emphasized the fact that being Christians means belonging to Christ. Just as the former illustration showed that the sheep in one stable belong to the farmer, the wife, by taking the husband's last name, belongs to the husband.

Caron's strong Reformed theology came to the foreground as he explained that the people of God who made up the whole church had been elected by God before the creation of the world.[76] God had elected or chosen these people for their eternal life. In time, when God saw fitting, he called the people to be gathered in the church by way of the calling through the preaching of his word and by the work of the Holy Spirit in the people's heart. Caron believed that election is not by chance. He believed that God already knew whom he would elect to eternal life from all eternity.[77]

Caron was against the view that saw God's electing people for salvation or damnation based on God's foreknowledge in eternity of whether or not the people would do good in time and therefore merit their salvation. In the sermon Caron did not use the technical terminology of foreknowledge. He merely stated that God's decision to elect and save was not based on God's preconceived knowledge that the elect would do good. He argued that good works and righteousness could only come from God, not from human beings. God will give the heavenly grace to whomever God decides to bestow it. God chooses his people because of God's own decision, and *God hardens the hearts of the people whom God wants to harden, and God loves those whom he wants to love.*[78] The italicized sentence was Caron's emphasis on the fact that God hardens the heart of those he wants to harden, and God loves those whom he wants to love. By printing this sentence in italic Caron sufficiently demonstrated that he believed in God sovereign decision in election and reprobation.

Caron followed the standard Reformed discussion on election and predestination. He quoted Paul who wrote that God has the sovereignty to do as he pleases. Caron took Paul's statement that the potter is free to create anything he wanted out of one lump of clay. The pottery does not have the

---

76. Caron, *Voorbeeldt des openbaeren Godtsdienst*, 45.
77. Caron, *Voorbeeldt des openbaeren Godtsdienst*, 46.
78. Caron, *Voorbeeldt des openbaeren Godtsdienst*, 46. Translation mine.

right or even the ability to protest to the potter why it is made the way the potter made it. In all God's decision, Caron said, God will be glorified. He believed that the mouths of the wicked would be shut tight because they would be ashamed of their own sins, and the members of the true church would praise God.

Caron believed that the church was started as God chose Seth, the son of Adam, to be the line of the chosen people. Through the line of the chosen people God continued to work, by raising the patriarch of Israel, until Jesus Christ came into the world. And since the time Christ ascended to heaven until the present time, and continuing to the end of the world, God keeps on gathering his people. Through the preaching of his word God calls people from all backgrounds—Islamic, pagan, and any other religious backgrounds—to be changed in their hearts and to follow Christ. Caron strongly believed that God is the only one who can change people's hearts, from their sinful devotion into righteousness in Christ. However, Caron also showed that people can only experience the change of their hearts after they hear the word of God. Therefore, Caron indicated that even though he strongly held on to the theology of election and predestination, he still saw the significance of the preaching of the gospel to all people. He did not rely on the doctrine of predestination as reason not to spread the gospel. Thus, we can see that in Caron—and we can also confidently say regarding other Reformed ministers in the East Indies—the urgency of preaching the gospel to all nations was ingrained in his calling as minister. Despite his strong belief in predestination, or perhaps because of his strong belief in predestination, Caron saw the urgency of preaching the gospel to all people. Thus, we can say that even though the Dutch ministers who were sent to the East Indies in the seventeenth century were not sent as missionaries in the strictest meaning of the word, they demonstrated the calling and the works of true missionaries in their effort to bring the gospel to the indigenous people.

The church will always last until the end of time. Caron believed that the Son of God will always reign over the church, despite the efforts of Satan to destroy the church. In the last part of his sermon Caron explicated his belief in the perseverance of the saints. He recognized that there were the enemies of the gospel who would take God's people away from him. However, Caron firmly believed that God would always keep his people safe in his hands. The enemy of the church, no matter how cunning he is, would never separate the church from her head, Jesus Christ.[79] Caron cited the suffering and persecution of people throughout the Old and New Testaments to show that even though God's people were persecuted, enslaved, exiled and even executed, God has never abandoned his people. And furthermore, Caron argued that the church of God has never been defeated by persecution.

Caron recognized that not all members of the visible, local church are the true members of the universal church. He reminded his audience that there might be hypocrites in the church. These hypocrites have received the same sign of baptism and parteken in the Lord's Supper, and thus they might look similar to the true believers. Interestingly, Caron used the imagery of fingernails and hair to illustrate these hypocrites. He said that even though nails and hair grow from the body, they are not the true parts of the body. People can cut their hair and nails without feeling pain in their body. Caron then used the opportunity to remind the people to do self-examination, to see if they truly believed in Jesus Christ as their Savior, and he also called the people to see if the Holy Spirit had truly changed their heart.

The juxtaposition between Caron's strong belief in the Reformed teaching of predestination and election and his repeated calling for the people to examine their own hearts and to keep on doing what is right according to the Scripture gives us some understanding of how Caron played his role as a minister. He repeatedly showed that the people must change their way of life, demonstrate the fruit of their repentance and live an upright life. These visible fruits must be evident in their lives because otherwise Christianity means nothing for them. At the same time, Caron also demonstrated that the repeated call to do good works was not a condition for their salvation, but good works should be the result that come out of a true relationship with God. In the context of the people in the East Indies, the fruit of their repentance needed to be made evident to show the rest of the community who did not believe in Christ that the believers were different, and therefore to be witnesses of the power of the gospel.

Caron continued his thoughts regarding election into the tenth sermon on the Apostles' Creed. He said that God had started the work of salvation for his people even before the creation of the world. He believed that God's election was not based on the goodness in human beings, but only out of his great love and mercy.[80] He reminded his listeners that all humans

---

79. Caron, *Voorbeeldt des openbaeren Godtsdienst*, 47.
80. Caron, *Voorbeeldt des openbaeren Godtsdienst*, 51.

have sinned in Adam, and therefore no one is free from sin. He used the Malay term *dosa pusaka* for "original sin." This term is still used in modern-day Malay and Indonesian languages to refer to original sin. He explained that the term *pusaka* Malay meant "inheritance." The reason why this term was suitable, he said, was because the original sin was like the inheritance that parents passed down to their children.

Anticipating some possible disagreement against the idea of original sin, Caron explained that all human beings have inherited the sin of Adam because Adam was the head and representative of all his descendants. He illustrated his view by saying that when a king has made a wrong decision, all the citizens of the kingdom also have to carry the consequence of the king's mistake. But then he continued by saying that people do not just have the original sin, but each person has also committed actual sin in their own lives. Therefore, he said, humans can only rely on Christ for forgiveness of sin. He told his audience that Christ has paid our debt of sin in full, and therefore there iss no more punishment for those whose sin God has forgiven. The benefit of Christ has not just been given to his people in the form of forgiveness of sins, Caron continued. God also has given his people another gift, namely the gift of sanctification of the Holy Spirit, so that the Holy Spirit cleanses his people from sins, changes their hearts and therefore the hearts of God's people are fully clean.

Caron's statement of double grace in the form of forgiveness of sin or justification and sanctification sounds very similar to Calvin's view of justification and sanctification. Calvin explicitly called the salvific work of Christ a "double grace" because in giving the grace of salvation God bestows both justification and sanctification. In Calvin's thought justification and sanctification are always linked together.[81] As a Reformed preacher, Caron demonstrated that he adopted similar view that Calvin had expounded, even though Caron did not use the theological terminology in his sermon.

The hope of resurrection should be the greatest hope for God's people. Caron wanted his readers to understand this truth. The biblical teaching of resurrection, Caron believed, functions as the foundation for our hope of eternal life, as well as comfort for those who suffer in this world. Resurrection will be the greatest reward for people who have suffered in the present world without ever experiencing the release that they expected. In the end, God will show his people that the reward has been waiting for them in

---

81. Calvin, *Institutes*, 3.11.1.

The Sermons of Franchois Caron as Further Reinforcement

eternity, and eternal life will be the greatest experience for the people, while eternal punishment and suffering will be waiting for the wicked.

Caron openly criticized other religions' teaching about life after death. He attacked Hindu believers in their idea of reincarnation. He stated that the idea of reincarnation is against the biblical teaching of resurrection, because Hinduism taught that the soul will be reincarnated into a different human person after the current person dies. He said that Islam was wrong in its belief that the souls of dead people can be seen in graveyards, and the souls of the departed would face two dark angels in the grave. More bitterly, Caron attacked the Roman Catholic doctrine of purgatory. He said that the idea of purgatory, a middle place in between hell and heaven, is not biblical.[82]

Following the testimony of the four Gospels regarding the resurrection of Jesus, Caron explained the reality of believers' resurrection. He said that Jesus was resurrected in his own body, not using another person's body. The resurrected body of Jesus, he believed, was real resurrection in flesh. Jesus' resurrection became the source and clearest demonstration of our resurrection. Caron emphasized that Jesus, the head of the church, had been resurrected, and it follows naturally that the members of Christ's body will also be resurrected in the end time. In explaining the resurrection Caron simply followed the Augustinian and Reformed view of resurrection, in that the soul, which is for a period of time separated from the body at physical death, will be reunited with the body. He said that on the second coming of Christ, the soul of the believers in heaven and the souls of the damned in hell will be joined to their bodies again, and all will stand before the Great Judge. Following Jesus' teaching in Matthew 25, Caron said that the resurrected people will stand on the left and on the right sides of Jesus. Then, Jesus the Great Judge will finally declare that the righteous will live forever with God, and the wicked will be punished eternally. And in the end, Caron concluded, the righteous will rejoice in the perfection that God has prepared for them.

Caron used the opportunity in the sermon on the resurrection of the body to call people to repentance. As it was also seen in his other sermons, Caron invited people to accept Jesus as their Savior so that they could have the eternal life and could experience the greatest joy of resurrection. He likened the new heaven and the new earth to the life that Adam and Eve knew in paradise before they fell into sin. This particular sermon sounds

---

82. Caron, *Voorbeeldt des openbaeren Godtsdienst*, 57.

like an evangelistic campaign to invite people to leave the life of sin and to come to salvation in Christ. This is another instance where even though Caron was a Reformed minister who believed in God's eternal predestination, he still made the outward calling to people to come to God and repent. Caron knew that he also had the task of bringing the gospel to everyone and outwardly challenged people to make the decision to come to Christ, even though, as was evident in the other parts of his sermons, he also believed that salvation started from God in eternity, and not in human's decision to accept or reject the offer of salvation.

In his own cultural and ecclesial context, Caron disagreed with Hinduism's practice of cremation. He believed that burial is the only acceptable way to treat the bodies of the deceased. He did not provide an elaborate theological foundation for his disagreement of cremation. He only said that the Old Testament people clearly buried their dead.[83] He also said that because the Bible said we are dust and we must return to dust, we must therefore bury the bodies of the dead. At the same time, however, he also acknowledged that there were people who have died in the sea, or in war or in terrible fire. In that case, he understood that the living can do nothing to the dead bodies. People could rely on the joy of resurrection that the souls of these people would also be reunited with their bodies, regardless of the cause of physical death. He only said that in the most ideal situation, and when a person dies in the home, the body should be buried. Caron's attack on the Hindu practice of cremation is an example of an attack against another religion that was not fully biblically and theologically grounded. Caron was being oppositional because he wanted to place Reformed Christianity over against other religions. Because he had a mission to convince the new believers in Ambon that Reformed Protestantism is the only true religion, he took the opportunity to attack and criticize cremation. In order to show that the Hindus did not get their theology right, he pointed out to the practice of cremation and just plainly called it wrong. Caron's view could have been shaped by his European background as well. He was perhaps unfamiliar with the practice of cremation when he studied in the Netherlands.

Caron further elaborated his view on eschatology in the last sermon on the Apostles' Creed. The belief in life everlasting, he said, also carries with it a promise that we would see God. For him, seeing God in the everlasting life meant that we will experience the greatness and kindness and

---

83. Caron, *Voorbeeldt des openbaeren Godtsdienst*, 60.

mercy of God in all its fullness.[84] He also emphasized the perfection of the believers in eternal life. He saw that sin will be no more, and the human heart and mind will be completely purified. He interpreted the biblical statements regarding heaven and eternal life as metaphors of the greatest joy that heaven could give to God's people.[85] The joy of heaven, he said, will also include real communion with God the Trinity, while at the same time people will recognize each other again—family members and friends, as well as the people in the Old and New Testaments. Caron's explanation of eternal life did not make clear distinction between the intermediate state of souls while waiting for the second coming of Christ and the resurrection of the body in the second coming of Christ. He focused his sermon on the idea of heaven and the blissfulness of heaven.

In harmony with what he wrote in the small catechism, *De Wegh na den Hemel*, Caron showed that Christianity is the only way to heaven. He ended his sermon on the Apostles' Creed with another call for people to leave their sinful way of life and to come to Christ who is the only Savior. He also comforted his audience by saying that for those who believed there is no greater joy than in anticipating entering eternal life in Christ.

---

84. Caron, *Voorbeeldt des openbaeren Godtsdienst*, 62.
85. Caron, *Voorbeeldt des openbaeren Godtsdienst*, 63.

4

Intersection of Doctrine and Christian Conducts in Caron's Sermons on the Ten Commandments and the Lord's Prayer

Caron Sermons on the Ten Commandments

CARON'S SERMONS ON THE Ten Commandments took a slightly different approach than the sermons on the Apostles' Creed. While in his sermons on the creed were mainly focused on teaching the basics of the doctrines of the Reformed church, the sermons on the Ten Commandments were clearly geared towards teaching the people how to live the Christian life. One noticeable difference in the sermons on the Ten Commandments was the part where he applies the teaching of the Bible in people's lives. In the sermons on the Ten Commandments Caron often challenged his readers to do certain deed or to take certain actions in their daily lives to apply the teaching of the Ten Commandments in their daily experience. This call for action was more applicable to the people than the applications Caron gave in his sermons on the creed, where he mostly repeated himself by calling people to love God more because God has done so much for them. Or, if there was any practical application that Caron called people to do in their lives, in the sermons on the creed he mostly called people to repent and leave their sinful way of life.

Following the custom already established by his predecessors, Caron used the Malay word *penjouruan* as the translation of "commandment." In the Malay-Dutch dictionary that Wiltens and Danckaerts compiled, the

Intersection of Doctrine and Christian Conducts in Caron's Sermons

word *penjouroan* was interpreted as *bevelen ende gebieden met macht ende autoriteyt*, or "to order or to command with strength and authority."[1] As the name "commandments" implied, the Ten Commandments were introduced to the people in the East Indies as series of order that God gave to his people by his authority and power as the God of the universe. Caron took the Ten Commandments very seriously, and in the sermons he often made repeated callings for the people to obey the Ten Commandments.

In his collection of sermons Caron gave a new title for the sermons on the Ten Commandments as: *Verklaringe en Toe-Eyegeninge der Tien Geboden van de Wet Godes, Gestelt in Tien Praedicatien*.[2] Caron opened his sermon series on the Ten Commandments by calling people to live a holy life for God. He likened the Ten Commandments to a mirror. Through this mirror people could look at their own lives and discover that their faces were not clean. So he called the people to repent and return to God. In some ways Caron repeated what Calvin often wrote. The fascination with mirror seemed to be a common trend among the Reformed ministers in that time period. We see here that Caron repeated what he saw within his tradition. Caron further reminded his audience that human sinfulness was so bad and the Ten Commandments showed them their inability to be right with God. However, at the same time, the Ten Commandments also led people to God. He said that the Ten Commandments functioned like a pillar of light in front of the people, to lead them through the way that God wanted them to take. Indirectly, by using the metaphor of a pillar of fire Caron directed the people's attention to the history behind the Ten Commandments, when God led the Israelites through the wilderness by way of pillar of light at night.

Caron took Moses' authorship of the Pentateuch very seriously. As a minister who lived in the era before higher criticism, he did not debate that Moses was the author of the five books of the Old Testament commonly attributed to him. At the same time he also showed that revelation was a unique event. He recognized that God was the author of the Bible, but at the same time Moses was the human author who actually penned the words.[3]

Caron emphasized the significance of understanding the entire Ten Commandments as God's word. He believed that when in Exodus 20 God says, "I am the Lord your God," the Bible must have meant that God himself

---

1. Wiltens and Danckaerts, *Vocabularium*, 104.
2. Hereafter: Caron, *Verklaringe*, followed by folio number.
3. Caron, *Verklaringe*, 3.

The Way to Heaven

spoke to Israel in an audible voice. He added that the thunder and cloud and lightning were the indications that the voice of God was literally heard by the people. This belief helped him to validate the significance of the Ten Commandments for the people who lived in the seventeenth-century East Indies. If God directly spoke to the Israelites using and audible, mysterious voice, the people in his days should also listen to the Ten Commandments attentively and obey them fervently.

God's personal introduction to the Israelites when he said "I am the Lord your God" indicated that God cared about his people. Caron emphasized that God's love and care to the people was clearly demonstrated in his redemptive work. God could have thrown all sinners to eternal damnation. But God still showed his mercy to his people, and he was even willing to make a covenant with them to be their Lord and their God.[4] He told the people that this great and magnificent Creator of heavens and earth was willing to enter into a covenantal relationship with the people. Therefore, the people must respond to God by showing reference and fear of the Lord.

Caron stated that the first commandment said that the people should not have other gods before the true God took the second-person singular pronoun "you." Caron pointed out that in Malay the second-person singular and second-person plural pronouns were signified by two different words. The Ten Commandments, he reminded the people, took the singular form, to show the people that each person was to respond individually to God by not worshipping any other gods. This reminder was important for the indigenous people of the East Indies, because they were surrounded by several religions. There were many syncretistic practices that Christians in the archipelago saw. Tribal religions were mixed with Islam to form localized type of cultic worships. Thus, Caron strongly reminded that Christians should not have any other gods. He said that the covenantal bond between God and his people was like the marital relationship between one husband and one wife. Just like the husband only belongs to the wife and the wife to the husband, God's people should only have a relationship with God, their Lord.

In the first sermon Caron used the opportunity to show the falsehood of other religions. In addition to criticizing Hinduism's problem of worshiping multiple gods, he also explicitly showed that the Chinese people were wrong in having shrines in their homes and used josh sticks to worship their ancestors. Caron also reminded the Ambonese that many of the

---

4. Caron, *Verklaringe*, 4.

people worshiped the sky or the earth. He also went far to say that the God of the Islamic people, who was also called Allah, was not the true God. This sermon sounded like an attack to other religions outside of Christianity. Caron was very serious in telling the people that Christians should only worship the one true God of the Bible, because he must have seen how complex religious lives in the East Indies had been. In a land where the people were not sufficiently instructed in the knowledge of religion, religious syncretism, just as other types of assimilations could easily happen. In order to maintain the purity of the Christian faith Caron saw it as his responsibility to teach the people. He also explicitly charged the Ambonese, that those who confessed Christianity but still held on to their tribal beliefs were guilty of trespassing the first commandment.

In the sermons on the Ten Commandments Caron spent more time teaching the people what to do in their daily lives as Christians. Caron told the people that keeping the first commandment also meant not placing anything else between God and themselves. This included the way the people look at money or wealth. Being stingy with their money, he told his audience, was as sinful as being greedy, because both actions placed money as the center of their lives, instead of having God as their only focus of devotion. Drunkenness, according to him, was also a trespass against the first commandment, because it meant that the drunkards found alcohol as the center of their lives, which should have been occupied by God. He then argued that visiting witch doctors or diviners for spiritual protection or method to gain wealth was also a form of having another god before the true God, and therefore it was equally sinful. In this sermon Caron showed good understanding of his audience's daily lives. These specific, pointed reminders of certain sins were indications that the people were familiar with these acts, and quite possibly Caron had seen some of the people do the acts. Therefore he explicitly mentioned them in the sermon and called for the people to take action.

Caron was particularly against the practice of witchcraft. He plainly said that witchcraft was equal to worshipping Satan, or more accurately, making a covenant with Satan. By using the term "covenant" Caron clearly made the comparison between the Ten Commandments as covenant with God and witchcraft as covenant with Satan. Beyond just sinning against God by turning their hearts to Satan, Caron pointed out that witchcraft, especially when the people visited witch doctors to gain wealth for themselves by way of injuring others or causing other people's businesses or livelihood

The Way to Heaven

to fail so that they could be richer, was a sin against others. Caron reminded them that in the Old Testament the prophets continuously rebuked the people who practiced witchcraft.[5] In this part of the sermon Caron used many biblical stories that focused on witchcraft and Satan worshipping, including the story of Jannes and Jambres, Saul's visit to the witch of En-Dor, Moses' fight against the magicians of Pharaoh, and many other stories. Caron listed one biblical story after another to make his point, and his way of telling the stories suggested that he knew that the people were also familiar with the Bible. What Caron said in the sermons was an indication that by the second half of the seventeenth century Christians in the East Indies were already familiar with most of the Bible. Caron's sermon, therefore, further demonstrated that the teaching of the Bible had reached a wide audience, including people in the rural areas. At the same time, his repeated reminders that the people should turn from their sinful ways might also be an indication that despite their knowledge of the biblical stories—or more widely, the teaching of the Reformed church—the people still had difficulty in applying the teaching in their lives.

In keeping with the Reformed church's rejection of anything superstitious, Caron said that people could be misled into thinking that certain action or rituals, when done within the context of worship, could result in some supernatural benefit for the people. He used the mistakes of the Pharisees as his example. The Pharisees, he said, put the emphasis on washing their hands and feet, as though these washing rituals could sanctify the hearts of the people. In the same breath he also pointed out to certain practices of the Roman Catholics, whom he called "the people of the Papisto." He said that the Roman Catholics believed the lighting of candles, the bread used in the Lord's Supper, the water used in baptism, a piece of wood from certain cross, the sound of bells, etc. could be used to do exorcism, or had the power to forgive sins and to cleanse the soul. He also criticized the Roman Catholics' practice of praying to saints, or to angels, and plainly told the people that these practices were against the first commandment.[6]

Caron's critique of local practices continued with what he noticed among the Ambonese when he was still with them, including the people's superstitious beliefs of carrying certain written magic formula in their pockets or in a pocket hung around their necks to cure them or prevent them from certain illnesses. He also rebuked the people who brought good

---

5. Caron, *Verklaringe*, 6.
6. Caron, *Verklaringe*, 8.

food to the graveyard of their ancestors as an offering to them in order that the dead ancestors would bless them. He also said that people's superstitious beliefs that if they accidentally kicked the front door of their houses on their way to work meant bad luck, but seeing a spider on their front door meant good luck were all equally unacceptable in light of God's word. In this sermon Caron demonstrated his deep understanding of what was going on in his audience's lives, and his true longing for a radical change in their daily practices.

Caron's effort to bring the people into the acceptable practice and conducts of Christianity showed similarity with what happened at the time of the Reformation in Europe about a century before. In Geneva, Calvin worked very hard to eradicate any superstitious practices that were rooted in medieval culture and the teaching of the church of Rome.[7] While the particular forms of superstitious beliefs and practices may be different from that of the European people, the ones practiced in the East Indies had the root of superstition in common. Caron wanted all forms of superstition to be eliminated from the lives of all Christians.

True worship must be directed to the Trinity: Father, Son and Holy Spirit. In line with the translation of the Heidelberg into Malay done by Danckaerts, Caron consistently used the name *Bappa* for God the Father, *Anac* for the Son and *Ruah Ulkadus* for the Holy Spirit.[8] In the sermons on the Ten Commandments Caron kept on emphasizing the significance of worshipping the Trinitarian God. He did not go into detail explaining the nature of the Trinity, since he already did it in his sermons on the Apostles' Creed. However, he was consistent in showing that the three persons of the Trinity are not three gods, but one God. And at the same time, Caron was also quick in pointing out the problems with the Ambonese's pagan rituals in which the people worshipped too many gods.

Caron was careful to distinguish worshipping idols in the forms of statues, pictures and other human creations from enjoying and appreciating arts. He was aware that many of the Ambonese were good at painting, wood carving and many other forms of fine art. He told the people that these art works were good and there was nothing wrong with producing them. He pointed out that many of the white people were also good at producing art works. But in keeping with the Ten Commandments, he reminded the

---

7. See, for instance, Calvin, *Institutes*, 4.7.22–24, 27.
8. Caron, *Verklaringe*, 10 and passim.

people that these art works were not to be worshipped.⁹ While appreciating art works for the sake of art, Caron said that there should not be any pictures or statues inside the church. He attacked the Portuguese's—the Roman Catholics'—use of the crucifix inside the church buildings. He openly attacked the Roman Catholics by saying that the crucifix was just a mute form of art that did not have any meaning. It cannot teach the people any true Christan doctrine. He insisted that the only important element in Christian worship was the preaching of the word of God. It is God's words that would help the people grow in their understanding of God.¹⁰

Caron charged Islam as false religion, and thus committing sin against the true God, because Islam insisted that Mohammad was greater than Jesus Christ. Caron also attacked the rituals and other believes of Islam, such as the washing ritual before praying in the mosque, fasting during the month of Ramadhan, its idea of clean and unclean food, circumcision for boys, pilgrimage to Mecca, and burial ritual that he considered superstitious.¹¹ Caron's critique of Islam gives us a way to look at how Islam had been practiced in the East Indies at the time when the Dutch Reformed churches were transplanted there. The religious practices of Islam that Caron criticized in his sermon were already an established system in the seventeenth century. By comparing what Caron mentioned in the sermon and what the Islamic communities are doing today, we can say that these Islamic rituals remain unchanged throughout the centuries.

Syncretism seemed to be a big issue that still lingered in Ambon at the time when Caron was a minister there. He pointed out that Christians should never mix the true teaching of the church—the Reformed church—with the pagan religion, Islam, and even with the superstitions of the Papists. Various syncretistic practices that Caron criticized included the requirements for boys to be circumcized as the entered puberty, the view that women were unclean during menstrual period, making the sign of the cross before praying, and inserting frankincense into the hand of a dead person before burial.¹² He insisted that Christians should only serve the true God without being burdened by these superstitious and syncretistic practices. Keeping the second commandment, he emphasized, meant that Christians only do what Scripture tells them to do. These syncretistic prac-

9. Caron, *Verklaringe*, 11.
10. Caron, *Verklaringe*, 11.
11. Caron, *Verklaringe*, 12.
12. Caron, *Verklaringe*, 12.

tices demonstrated that the people still did not worship the only one God of the Bible. And together with his critique of syncretism, Caron also showed that living morally upright as Christians was a demonstration that people kept God's commands. He rebuked those who were slothful, easily angered, addicted to alcohol, dishonest and gluttonous and called them to repent. This rebuke indicated that there were still people who did not follow the teaching of the church for them to live morally. Since the Reformed church insisted on morality, and even the church order required that the ministers maintained the discipline in the church, Caron saw the necessity to call people to repentance. The sermon on the second commandment of the Ten Commandments became a good avenue for him to educate and remind the people of what they must or must not do.

Knowing that his published sermons would be read by non-ordained church workers such as the comforters of the sick and school teachers, Caron reminded these church workers to be diligent in their works and to be examples for others. When they remind lay people to flee away from idol worship, they must first apply the principle to their own lives. He explicitly addressed these church workers in the sermon, reminding them that they must bring the teaching of true Christianity, to fight against Islam and other false religions, at school and in the church.[13] Idol worship was abomination in the eyes of God, and all Christians must get rid of these idols. Caron noticed that many people still kept idols in their houses, and therefore he urged the church workers to keep reminding people to throw away these idols from their houses.

Caron's sermons may also function as a lens for us today to see what was going on in the lives of Christians in the East Indies in the seventeenth century. There was a sense that the indigenous people resisted the sacraments because they thought that the sacraments were just a custom or tradition. Some of these people seemed to deny the significance of the sacraments because they did not understand the meaning of the sacraments. In his sermon on the third commandment, when he explained the meaning of not using the name of the Lord in vain, Caron stated that those who did not value the sacraments and reject the significance of the sacraments had also fallen into the sin of using the name of the Lord in vain, because they have looked down upon the sacraments that the Lord has instituted for the people.[14] Therefore Caron explained that keeping and celebrating the sacra-

13. Caron, *Verklaringe*, 14.
14. Caron, *Verklaringe*, 19.

The Way to Heaven

ments were significant for the spiritual lives of the people. By partaking in the sacraments the people proclaim Jesus Christ until he comes again. Thus, keeping the sacraments also meant not using the name of the Lord in vain.

Very often Caron reminded Christians in the East Indies that they had to keep the Sabbath. In his sermon on the fourth commandment he was very careful in showing that there was a shift from the Old Testament practice of keeping the Sabbath on Saturday to Christians' practice of keeping the Sabbath on Sunday. The resurrection of Jesus is the reason why Christians worship God on Sunday.[15] By the time the Dutch came to the archipelago the Portuguese and the Jesuit missionaries had already spread the teaching of Roman Catholicism to many of the people in the archipelago. Caron explained that the people had adopted the name "Domingo" to refer to the seventh day. He said that the Portuguese word literally means "the day of the Lord."[16] Here we see that the Portuguese language and culture was adopted just as it was in the Protestant circle. Caron and other Dutch ministers did not need to fight regarding the name of the seventh day. The Portuguese word *Domingo* fits just fine to refer to the day, and the East Indian people were accustomed to calling the day Domingo, therefore they could continue with the custom. The meaning of Domingo as "the day of the Lord" already helped the people to know the significance of Sunday for their Christian life and worship, therefore, it was fine for the people to continue using the name. Even today, the Indonesian word for Sunday, *Minggu*, is derived from the Portuguese name for the day.

God's command to rest on the seventh day meant, according to the Reformed tradition, rest from work. Caron made this command sound very simple and understandable for the people. He said that on Sunday people should refrain from doing their daily activities, from trading, from selling and buying, from working in their fields, from fishing, from weaving cloths, and they must go to church.[17] His sermon was also directed toward the VOC's workers. He said that company workers should not use Sundays to do other works to earn some extra income and skip going to church. At the same time, he also reminded the people that they should not fall into the traps of the Pharisees who were legalistic. He listed activities that were allowed to be conducted on Sundays, which included having the company

15. Caron, *Verklaringe*, 26.
16. Caron, *Verklaringe*, 26.
17. Caron, *Verklaringe*, 26.

Intersection of Doctrine and Christian Conducts in Caron's Sermons

of friends to enjoy meals together and to discuss what the minister said in the sermon, having good talk with others to build their faith and to encourage each other, and doctors and other people who worked to help alleviate the suffering of the people should also continue their work on Sundays. And just like what Chrrist said to the Jews, the people were not forbidden to help or rescue animals that needed help.[18] In his sermon on keeping the Sabbath, Caron brought the significance of rest and worship to the level that the people could understand and keep, and at the same time he also showed that Sabbath should give freedom and joy to the people, and not restrictions.

Caron nicely weaved the fifth commandment, "honor your father and your mother," together with Jesus' command to love one's neighbors as oneself. He stated that the first step in loving one's neighbors was by honoring one's parents. In keeping with the Reformed tradition, at the beginning of his fifth sermon on the Ten Commandment he also explained that the Ten Commandments were divided into two tables: the first table, which contained the first four commandments, dealt with God, and the second table dealt with human beings. The commandment to honor father and mother stood at the very first line on the second table.[19] Also in keeping with the Reformed teaching expressed in the Heidelberg Catechism,[20] he explained that honoring one's father and mother went beyond one's biological parents. The commandment also meant, he said, that people are all called to respect and honor anybody that has authority above us. Caron spelled out that in the civil society respect and honor must be directed to political leaders, kings, governors etc., in the church due respect and honor must be given to ministers, elders and school teachers, and at home respect and honor must be given to father and mother, or whoever is in charge of taking care the children.[21]

While explicating what the Reformed church believes and teaches regarding the fifth commandment, Caron also gently advanced the insistence that the people in the East Indies should obey authority. As the Dutch were gaining more and more power over the archipelago, there was also the need for them to establish their authority. Thus, Caron's sermons could work as another push to ensure that the indigenous people would be willingly

18. Caron, *Verklaringe*, 26.
19. Caron, *Verklaringe*, 29.
20. Heidelberg Catechism, question and answer 104.
21. Caron, *Verklaringe*, 30.

submissive to the Dutch. At the same time, Caron's sermons also pointed out the need of the people to obey leaders in the church. As we have seen in the way the church orders were composed, leadership in the church included ministers, elders and teachers. By explicitly stating their authority in the church in this sermon, Caron was making sure that order in the church could also be maintained. What we see in Caron's sermon here confirms Robert Bast's view that this commandment had been used to instruct and enforced obedience to the traditional leaders of the household, the leaders of the church and the political leader. This insistence, Bast explains, had been imposed at least since the thirteenth century.[22] For the Dutch in the East Indies, Caron's sermons had an added benefit to ensure complete obedience to the new rulers. As the VOC was establishing its authority in the archipelago, people's complete obedience to the Dutch based on such religious teaching would seal the strong authority that the Dutch had over the lay people.

To make his sermon applicable to his readers, Caron carefully explained the proper, Christian way of maintaining relationships between parents and children, leaders and members of the community, and church leaders and lay people in the congregation.[23] Caron stated that parents have worked hard and sacrificed significantly for the good of their children. Therefore, children must honor their parents according to God's word. At the same time, he also called parents to their obligation to send their children to school to be taught the right teaching of the church. Caron clearly brought the strong intention of the Dutch to teach the young in the knowledge of the Reformed teaching in this sermon. As the sermon would be read by other church workers in different churches in the remote villages, this exhortation would then reach a wider audience so that more and more parents would send their children to schools to be catechized. Thus, Caron's sermon functioned well as a tool to spread the expectations of the Dutch to instill the knowledge of Reformed doctrines into the minds of the people.

While Caron called people to obey political leaders, governors and kings, he also reminded these leaders to ensure that they bring the truth of God's words to the people. They must protect people and help people to flourish so that they become worthy of the obedience and honor they deserve.[24] Similarly, he showed that ministers were worthy of respect and

---

22. Bast, *Honor Your Fathers*, 44.
23. Caron, *Verklaringe*, 30.
24. Caron, *Verklaringe*, 32.

honor, because they brought God's word to the people. They also served the congregation with all their heart, mind and soul. These ministers were called to be the leaders and examples for the people in how they should worship God and obey God. In their leadership, ministers had to devote their own lives to make sure that the teachings of Christ would be rooted in the lives of the believers. Therefore, the ministers should be properly respected.[25] Then, Caron exhorted little children to be obedient to their school teachers and to listen to their teaching well. In addition, he forbade the children from falsely reporting the school teachers to their parents, as though the teachers had performed bad deeds.[26] From what Caron wrote in the sermon we can see that there were probably cases in which children were reluctant to go to school, and therefore they made false reports to their parents regarding their children so that they did not have to go to school. To these school children Caron said that when they disobeyed their teachers at school and made such false reports they sinned against the fifth commandment.

Caron distinguished killing and murder clearly in his sermon on the sixth commandment. He stated that in the Old Testament, when the Israelites went into war they had to kill their enemies, because God told them so. Thus, he reminded his audience that not all actions of taking other people's lives were sinful.[27] He also mentioned that in the current time, kings and leaders sometimes had to take up their weapons to defend their countries and to drive away their enemies. Similarly, he believed that a person defending his or her own house from burglars and robbers might at times take up weapons and kill the invaders. These actions, in his opinion, were not sins against the sixth commandment. What would be a sinful act of murder, he then stated, was the act of taking the lives of people out of one's own hatred, anger, or jealousy. He took actual examples that might very well be common in the lives of the Ambonese, where people poisoned others, or slain others with sword or lancet to gain profit from their deaths. He also said that it was equally sinful to pay people to murder other people.

Caron's careful distinction between killing and murder might have been beneficial for the Dutch in the context of colonization. The Dutch had been in wars with the Portuguese and various indigenous groups in the East Indies as they established their rule in the land. If it was true that

25. Caron, *Verklaringe*, 33.
26. Caron, *Verklaringe*, 33.
27. Caron, *Verklaringe*, 36.

the Dutch killed people out of necessity of self-defense and to maintain order, then the killing of the indigenous people or perhaps other nations such as the Portuguese could be justified. But one could argue that Caron's sermon could also function as a convenient statement or teaching to defend what the Dutch did in order to gain a monopoly on spice trading in the archipelago. In the sermon Caron did not emphasize too heavily on the issue and neither did he use the Dutch as an example. But when one reads his sermon in the context of colonization, one would naturally be led into thinking about the possibility of Caron's use of the sermon to defend the Dutch.

Obedience to the sixth commandment also included refraining from committing suicide. Caron was very graphic and to the point in telling people that Christians should not commit suicide either by hanging themselves, or cutting their own vein, or slashing one's own throat or jumping into deep water.[28] These actions might have been the ones that people in the area had done when they committed suicide. He openly charged that committing suicide was the work of Satan. He believed that those who decided to take their own lives had allowed Satan to enter their heart, so that instead of having hope and trust in God they succumbed to Satan's teaching of hopelessness and despair.[29] Another practical application of the commandment was to refrain from cursing other people and calling other people bad names, and to abuse others verbally, to lash out anger toward other people. He plainly said that such verbal abuse was equal to murdering others.[30] Conversely, the commandment called people to uphold other people's lives and to live in love and peace with each other. Christians should flee from hatred and passion to cause harms to others, he said, and they should seek peace with one another.[31]

Caron's thoughts on practical application of his sermons on the Ten Commandments went beyond the surface values of doing and refraining from doing certain actions. He included motivations, thoughts and meditations of the heart as parts of what Christians must consciously take into consideration when trying to keep the Ten Commandments. In teaching the people of how to keep the seventh commandment, Caron said that the command not to commit adultery included in it God's call to free ourselves

28. Caron, *Verklaringe*, 37.
29. Caron, *Verklaringe*, 38.
30. Caron, *Verklaringe*, 39.
31. Caron, *Verklaringe*, 40.

from all kinds of impurities that would cause sexual immorality through actual sinful acts, filthy speech and inner lust.[32] Then he explained that the seventh commandment distinguished the difference between adultery and fornication. Adultery, according to him, was extra-marital sex done by two married people. He saw this as a "double-layered" sin, because each sinful party sommitted wrongdoing to their own spouse and the other party's spouse. Fornication, in his mind, was a "one-layered" sin, because this act was committed by unmarried people.[33] He also reminded people that committing adultery was wrong not only because it was forbidden by God but also because it could potentially hurt the children that would be born out of this sinful act. The illegitimate children born out of such relationship, he reminded his audience, would have to carry the shame for their entire lives. Therefore, faithful Christians should never commit this serious sin.

In Caron's mind, the religion of Islam was misguided in allowing men to have multiple wives. Caron used the opportunity to criticize Islam as he explained how the seventh commandment was very good and beneficial to keep healthy marital relationships for Christians. In his typical fashion of being confrontational, he openly charged the Muslims as having fallen into the mistake of Muhammad who taught that it was fine for men to have multiple wives, provided that he could be just to all his wives.[34] Caron attributed permission to be polygamous as part of the reason why Islam and paganism were still the religions of the majority of the people. He reasoned that because men could have multiple wives in Islam and in many of the tribal religions in Asia, and Christianity was so strict in imposing monogamy, Christianity was unpopular.[35]

The eighth commandment could be interpreted much wider than as just a prohibition from stealing. Caron creatively and carefully expanded the significance of keeping the commandment. On one level, he showed that the commandment meant that people should not take away other people's rightful possession. This included trying to take away people's possessions by way of tricks and dishonest manipulation.[36] On another level, stealing could also mean invading other people's territory. He said that this had been done by rulers of countries who took possession of the land

---

32. Caron, *Verklaringe*, 41.
33. Caron, *Verklaringe*, 41.
34. Caron, *Verklaringe*, 43.
35. Caron, *Verklaringe*, 44.
36. Caron, *Verklaringe*, 48.

that belonged to a different nation. Not paying taxes to the government, according to Caron, also fell into the category of trespassing the eighth commandment. To make his sermon applicable to the Ambonese, most of whom were sailors or closely connected to sea-faring lives, he stated that pirates were prime examples those who sin against the eighth commandment. The commandment not to steal also included, in Caron's explanation, prohibition to cheat or be dishonest in measurement, performing usury and gambling. He often cited the books of Leviticus and Deuteronomy to demonstrate that the Old Testament had provided clear direction for people to live honestly and to prevent people from taking advantage from others, especially those who were in a much weaker position than themselves.[37]

Christians were called to follow what Jesus taught in Matthew 7, Caron said, and therefore people must do unto others what they want others to do unto them.[38] The implication of Jesus' teaching and the eighth commandment was that Christians are called to help others in any way they can, to ensure that others may have a good life, which also includes having enough means to support themselves. This also meant that Christians have the responsibility to improve the life of society, and to protect each other's possessions in the comunity so that nobody would steal from each other. At the same time, this commandment also meant, for Caron, that people are called to work hard and to help the poor in the society.[39]

There is a close connection among all the commandments in the Ten Commandments, and especially between the eighth and the ninth commandments. Caron explained the connection very well. At the beginning of his ninth sermon on the Ten Commandments, he stated that when people respect and honor other people's lives, and they work hard to ensure that others will live well and peacefully, they will also be free from all covetousness. Christians are called to keep the good names of others, he said, because, as Proverbs said, a good name is better than good oil.[40] Making false witnesses could appear in different forms, Caron explained, and certain people were vulnerable of committing such sins. Among other situations he mentioned judges who did not decide justly, people who said false and acrimonious statements against their neighbors, falsely charging others and

---

37. Caron, *Verklaringe*, 51.
38. Caron, *Verklaringe*, 53.
39. Caron, *Verklaringe*, 53.
40. Caron, *Verklaringe*, 54.

witnesses who told lies as the most serious examples of such sin.[41] He also openly said that verbal abuse, unjustly causing shame to others and telling people off in front of others also fell under the same category of trespassing the ninth commandment. Calling people names when quarelling with each other was also sin against the ninth commandment, Caron emphasized.[42]

Caron's sermons on the Ten Commandments demonstrated his heart as a pastor. Through exhortations, encouragements and rebukes he brought the message of the Bible to the level that his audience could understand. He cited many biblical passages in his sermons, even though at the time when he preached to the Ambonese the people still did not have the majority of the Bible translated into Malay. But his sermons could stand as a substitute of the Bible for the people. He started each sermon on the Ten Commandments with a quote on that particular commandment and proceeded with careful explanation of what the commandment meant. His sermons also give modern readers a sense of what happened in the society at that time. His practical applications of the teachings of the Bible and his rebukes of particular sins provide us today with some understanding of what the Ambonese—and quite likely the majority of the people in the East Indies—did or said or performed in their daily lives.

Caron's Sermons on the Lord's Prayer

Following his sermons on the Ten Commandments, Caron published a series of seven sermons based on the Lord's Prayer. In the 1693 reprint of the collection of Caron's sermons, these seven sermons directly followed the sermons on the Ten Commandments. Caron gave the title *Seven Praedicatien over 'tGebed des Heeren* for this collection of sermons.[43] In these sermons Caron showed a strong intention of teaching his audience several basic doctrines of the Reformed church. While he still kept his homiletical style which was rooted in the biblical text and applicable to the context of the Ambonese in the seventeenth century, he also used the opportunity in every sermon to explicate certain theological teachings of his church.

Caron started his first sermon on the Lord's Prayer with a very elaborate explanation on the doctrine of the Trinity. Partly repeating what he had explicated in his sermons on the Apostles' Creed, he stated that the

---

41. Caron, *Verklaringe*, 55.
42. Caron, *Verklaringe*, 56.
43. Hereafter: Caron, *Seven Praedicatien*, followed by page number.

Trinity has always been together. Jesus taught the disciples this prayer because in reality Jesus was always in communication with God the Father, in the power and presence of the Holy Spirit.[44] When we pray, he further said, we come to God our Father with the guidance of the Holy Spirit who enlightens our minds through Jesus Christ our Savior. Christians worship God our Father who is in heaven, he further stated, because God the Father listens to his children.

Even though the doctrine of the Trinity is a difficult doctrine to explain, Caron tackled the doctrine boldly. He explained that according to Scripture the Father as one divine person of the Trinity could be considered as the source of the divine nature. But at the same time, even when we address our prayer to God the Father, he reminded his audience that we must also think of the Son and the Holy Spirit as always together with the Father because the three are actually one.[45] In our prayer we address the Father, he explained, because the Father is the source, and he represents the whole divine nature in the Trinity.

The reason why God the father is called "Father" in Caron's mind was because Jesus the Son of God calls him Father. The reason why Jesus calls the Father as his Father, Caron further reminded the people, was because the name Father shows God's love and care and goodness, so that in calling him Father we too can be reminded that God has shown his goodness toward us.[46] This statement is consistent with what he already said in his sermons on the Apostles' Creed. And together with the concept of God's goodness, the name Father also showed people, according to Caron, that even when people sin they can always return to the Father, just like human fathers will receive their children even when the children have done something wrong. Caron connected the goodness and love of God the Father to the gift of redemption in Jesus Christ. His view of redemption in Christ was characteristically Reformed, in that he showed that sinners could only find justification through the work of Christ. In a strong Trinitarian fashion he then explained that the Holy Spirit is the one who opens people's hearts so that they could repent and come to God as redeemed people.[47]

Caron insisted that the pronoun used in the prayer is "ours," and not "my," first to show that Christians are in a community when they pray, and

---

44. Caron, *Seven Praedicatien*, 67.
45. Caron, *Seven Praedicatien*, 67.
46. Caron, *Seven Praedicatien*, 68.
47. Caron, *Seven Praedicatien*, 68.

Intersection of Doctrine and Christian Conducts in Caron's Sermons

also to show that this prayer teaches Christians not to be selfish. When we pray "Our Father" we automatically acknowledge that we share God the Father with others. This pronoun shows us that all believers are brothers and sisters in Christ, Caron said, and so, like what Paul said, we are all one family with one Father, and with one mother, the church, confessing one Lord and united in one baptism.[48]

Even when Jesus said that our Father is in heaven, it does not mean that God is locked in heaven, Caron explained. He explained the omnipresent nature of God in a very simple way by saying that God's presence is everywhere, in all his creation. But the word "heaven" points to the name and glory of God, power that God has over all the angels, and also the place where the souls of departed believers are now.[49] The holiness of God's name, in Caron's theology, first of all points to the character of God who is holy and separated from any other gods. But this separatedness of God, he further explained, also meant that God has separated ordinary objects and human experience into holy objects and experience. He particularly connected the first request in the Lord's Prayer, "hallowed be Thy name," with worship and sacrament. He said that because God is holy and people hallow the name of God, when Christians worship God on Sunday the ordinary day Sunday becomes a holy and separated day. Similarly, when infants are baptized the ordinary water becomes holy in the context of the sacrament, and the bread and wine which humans ordinarily consume at meals become holy and separated when used in the Lord's Supper.[50] The implication of God's holiness and humans' confession of hallowing the name of God also means that people must live a holy life. He exhorted Christians to have way of life that is different from non-believers. Being holy or separated means that they do not do what their non-believer neighbors do in their sinful, pagan way of life.

Confessing and proclaiming God's holy name should also bring Christians to praise God in all he has done in creation and providence. Repeating a similar theme as he had expanded in his sermons on the Apostles' Creed, Caron went back to his explanation of God's revelation in nature. To his Ambonese audience he showed how much God had done in creating beautiful islands, variety of trees, plants, flowers and spices that grew so well in the archipelago. He pointed out that God has created the heavens and the

---

48. Caron, *Seven Praedicatien*, 69.
49. Caron, *Seven Praedicatien*, 70.
50. Caron, *Seven Praedicatien*, 73.

earth with his great mind, and God continues to uphold and sustain his creation through the work of his providence.[51] In the sermon Caron did not use the word "providence," however, he comfortably explained what providence means. In a fashion very characteristic of Reformed theology, Caron kept showing that God's continuous care of the whole universe that he created shows that God has never departed from his creation.

Caron's second sermon on the Lord's Prayer is a wonderful example of a seventeenth-century sermon that easily combined deep doctrinal teaching with practical application. In this one sermon Caron was able to show his listeners the biblical teaching of God's work of creation and providence, human fall into sin, Christ's redemptive work and believer's responsibilities to serve and worship God as an act of praise and thanksgiving for God's work for them. He ended the sermon with an exhortation for the people to apply this teaching in their daily lives by loving God with all their heart, mind and might, and loving neighbors as themselves. Practically, he showed that loving God means praising God and upholding God's holy name in all that they do, not just at church, but in their daily lives. Serving God, he said, must also happen at home, where family members love each other. Serving God must also happen when people work in the fields or in the forest, in dealing with each other and in being just to each other.[52] Loving neighbors means that they must be good and caring to others, in words, acts and thoughts.[53] This sermon, therefore, became one of the tools that could serve as guidance for Christians in the archipelago to apply the teaching of the Bible in their daily experience. As this sermon got circulated in different parts of the archipelago, people who heard this could be educated in this type of Christian worldview, and thus transplantation of such worldview could start taking roots in the lives of the people.

The theme of praising and magnifying God's holy name continued to Caron's third sermon on the Lord's Prayer. The second petition in the prayer, "Thy kingdom come," said Caron, calls people to acknowledge that God's power and sovereignty are all over the earth. Since God's kingdom means God's power and authority, he explained, human beings must confess first of all that God is the creator of the universe, and particularly, in the redemptive relationship that humans have with God, redeemed people of God must also confess that Jesus has come into their hearts through the

---

51. Caron, *Seven Praedicatien*, 74.
52. Caron, *Seven Praedicatien*, 77.
53. Caron, *Seven Praedicatien*, 76.

Intersection of Doctrine and Christian Conducts in Caron's Sermons

power of the Holy Spirit.[54] Just like Calvin's thought on believers' union with Christ through the power of the Holy Spirit,[55] Caron's explanation on this petition right away brought people to the recognition that God's kingdom is already present in the lives of the believers, especially dwelling in the hearts of believers because they have been united with God in Christ. Christ is the King of all kings, he said, and therefore, when we are united with Christ we too have the benefits of living as the children of our King. Caron explained this teaching in very simple language that the Ambonese would be able to understand. He said that because Christ the King owns the entire universe his followers also have what Christ has. He carefully said that these are not worldly or physical possessions, but heavenly and spiritual, namely righteousness, peace and joy that Jesus gives to those who believe in him.[56]

Because God's gift in Christ is so great, and God's kingdom has come on earth, Caron also reminded the Christians in Ambon to advance God's teaching and to tell others who are still not believers to come to God through Christ. He brought his sermon into practical application of calling people to spread the Gospel.[57] He also pointed out that ministers and school teachers have done hard work in being obedient to God's call to spread the good news in the East Indies. Like in the sermon on the fifth commandment, he reminded his listeners that many Dutch ministers had left their home land and sacrificed their own lives to come to the Indies and teach the people God's word. They learned Malay so that they could preach and teach effectively, baptized children and adults, officiated the Lord's Supper, and do so many other ministerial duties in order that God's kingdom could continue to penetrate into the most remote areas in the Indies. Therefore, the people should also respect the ministers and school teachers while also trying to do some part of the work to teach each other as much as they could.[58]

Praying the Lord's Prayer requires believers to have a change of heart. When he explained the meaning of the third petition, "Thy will be done, on earth as it is in heaven," Caron first said that as long as people still follow their own will, or worse, they still follow Satan's will, they would never be

---

54. Caron, *Seven Praedicatien*, 79.
55. Calvin, Institutes, 3.1.1.
56. Caron, *Seven Praedicatien*, 81.
57. Caron, *Seven Praedicatien*, 82.
58. Caron, *Seven Praedicatien*, 83.

The Way to Heaven

able to worship God truthfully.[59] Caron believed that God's will has been with God from all eternity.[60] Whatever God wills, he said, will certainly come into reality. Praying that God's will be done on earth as it is in heaven, according to Caron, means that believers' requests that God would make to happen that God has decided or determined from eternity. Because God is the true God, God never changes or reverses what he has said. For his audience, Caron taught that the first thing to request God in following this petition is to pray that God would give his words to people and that people would understand God's words. The fruit of this petition would be people's changed hearts so that they would always follow God's words and commands.[61] Then, following the Heidelberg Catechism, he further explained that this petition meant that the believers ask God that they would reject their own will and obey God without protesting because God's will is the only one that is good.[62] Caron understood that human beings are weak, and it is always difficult for human beings to follow God's will. Therefore, the third petition directs people to ask for God's will to be done on earth as it is in heaven.[63]

The fourth petition in the Lord's Prayer, Caron explained, is focused on human physical needs. He said that the first three petitions lead people to ask for and think of spiritual needs, and now comes the fourth petition requesting God to bless his people with their physical needs. He used the word "bread" in his sermon, and showed that bread means all the body needs daily. The request for God to give his people their daily bread also included request for clothing, place to live, land that would produce good crops, safety in the land and at church, good fortune in one's daily job and protection from accidents.[64] In this sermon he carefully demonstrated that the fourth petition covers a wide range. This way he was able to teach the people that the prayer would help the people in their day-to day activities, in their most basic efforts to have a good life. He also made a point to show that the pronoun "our" is used in this petition so that people could understand that this prayer was intended as a communal prayer, that believers pray together for the common good of all people. The pronoun, he

---

59. Caron, *Seven Praedicatien*, 84.
60. Caron, *Seven Preadicatien*, 84.
61. Caron, *Seven Praedicatien*, 85.
62. Caron, *Seven Praedicatien*, 85; Heidelberg Catechism, question and answer 124.
63. Caron, *Seven Praedicatien*, 86.
64. Caron, *Seven Praedicatien*, 89.

said, would eliminate all selfish ambitions and self-centeredness. When Christians pray and ask this petition they are also called to think of the good of others. Another practical implication of this petition, Caron said, was that people should not be lazy. This prayer teaches that people must work, and as they work they ask for God's blessings so that they may have enough bread for the day.[65]

The fourth petition, according to Caron, also teaches people to be humble. As people know that it is God who blesses, and causes plants to grow, animals to multiply, and fish to fill the oceans, they will always be drawn to praise God and to be thankful for each blessing he has given to the people. This thankfulness, he said, would also remind people to stay away from dishonest living, and also from gambling.[66] Through reading Caron's sermon modern readers can see that Caron's rebuke indicated that some people in his time had the inclination to be dishonest and also to gamble. As gambling could be seen as the easiest short cut to earn as much money as possible with very litlle or no work at all, people were easily drawn to this activity. Caron seemed to be showing the people that the pious Christian life should be free from such an attitude, because all along his sermons had taught people to live an honest living, to rely on God for all blessings, and to seek the good of others, not just for themselves. Gambling was contrary to all that God's words had taught the people.

Caron returned to the call to repentance when he started his sixth sermon on the Lord's Prayer. He stated that the fifth petition acknowledges that we are all sinners and therefore we must ask God for forgiveness. He saw that the root of human sinfulness was the original sin that has been passed down from Adam to all his descendants, and therefore all people must repent to God. But at the same time he reminded his listeners that all people also commit their own individual sins beyond the original sin. Bringing together the message he had preached in the series of sermons based on the Ten Commandments, he plainly told people that we are indebted to God because of our sins.[67] Because sin is debt to God, he said, people must pay it back. Human beings cannot pay their own debt, but thankfully Jesus has come to complete the work of redemption. Therefore,

---

65. Caron, *Seven Praedicatien*, 90.
66. Caron, *Seven Praedicatien*, 90.
67. Caron, *Seven Praedicatien*, 94.

Caron called the people to continually ask for God's forgiveness because God always hears the prayers of his people, and he will forgive.[68]

Caron's sermon on the fifth petition had the evangelistic traits in it. He placed redemption in Christ at the center of his talk, and he repeated the passion narrative of the four Gospels to remind his readers of Christ's suffering for the forgiveness of humans' sins. Reciting John 3:16 in his sermon, he showed the people that pardon from sin is only possible because of God's love for the world, that he gave his Son so that those who believe in him shall not parish but have eternal life.[69] In Christ God has guaranteed forgiveness for sinners. But then, in a purely rhetorical style he asked the question of why people still have to ask for forgiveness if God has already forgiven their sins. His answer was twofold. First, people must ask for forgiveness because by asking they can know and feel that they are really forgiven. Secondly, every time Christians pray and ask for forgiveness they are to always remember Christ's death for the forgiveness of humans' sins.[70]

The petition to ask for God's forgiveness also brings believers to forgive others who have sinned against them. This petition, according to Caron, teaches believers not to repay evil for evil and not to look for the bad of others. But rather, people must have peace with each other. Because God has forgiven us, he said, we are called to forgive others. He told the listeners the parable of the ungrateful servant in Matthew 18. He retold the parable in its entirety without providing the biblical reference of the parable. He did it in a very effective way so that the retelling of the parable was clear and very vivid, and it must have worked for the audience to understand the meaning of the parable, namely that they must be willing to forgive others because they have received enormous forgiveness from God.[71]

Caron's last sermon on the Lord's Prayer focused on the sixth petition, "lead us not into temptation but deliver us from evil." Caron explained that there are two different kinds of temptation. The first one, which comes from God, is positive in nature because it comes in the form of testing. He illustrated this type of temptation with the image of a goldsmith purifying gold. When the gold is put in fire, all the impurities are taken out and the end result is pure gold that has a very high value.[72] He said that God's test-

68. Caron, *Seven Praedicatien*, 95.
69. Caron, *Seven Praedicatien*, 96.
70. Caron, *Seven Praedicatien*, 96.
71. Caron, *Seven Praedicatien*, 99.
72. Caron, *Seven Praedicatien*, 100.

Intersection of Doctrine and Christian Conducts in Caron's Sermons

ing of Abraham to sacrifice his son Isaac was this type of temptation. In the end it was Abraham's righteousness that came out as the result.

The second kind of temptation, according to Caron, is the one caused by Satan. Caron used the story of Job as the basis of his thought. He argued that Satan had caused Job all his suffering, because Satan wanted to cause Job all kinds of harm.[73] The Lord's Prayer helps believers to continually pray that this type of temptation would not come to them. Christians are called to ask for deliverance from evil. Caron simply stated that the word "evil" here refers to Satan.[74] The work of Satan causes people to sin, which will lead to punishment from God. But help is available from God. By asking to be delivered from evil Christians request that God will intervene and actively shelter the believers from Satan. Caron called his listeners to ask repeatedly that they may be delivered from evil, because Satan works unceasingly. But thanks to God, his power is always there to defeat Satan.[75]

Caron ended his sermon series on the Lord's Prayer with a high note of hope that God hears his children's prayer. He explained that the word "amen" at the end of the prayer meant that what the people say and pray about are true. Explaining the meaning of the word from its Hebrew origin, he told the people that "amen" means, in Malay, *sesongo* and *sabenar*.[76] These two Malay words are synonymous with each other, and both mean "truly." So, by using these two synonymous words together he wanted to emphasize the meaning of the word "amen" that there is truth and guarantee in the meaning of the word.

Caron did not include the conclusion of the Lord's Prayer, "for thine is the kingdom, and the power and the glory forever," in his sermon. He just followed the shorter ending of the prayer without giving any explanation that there is a variant in the ending. In this case he did not follow the Heidelberg Catechism, which includes the conclusion of the prayer.[77] The absence of the conclusion of the prayer in the series of sermon is curious, because in his Malay translation of *De Wegh na den Hemel* he included the long ending of the prayer.[78]

---

73. Caron, *Seven Praedicatien*, 101.
74. Caron, *Seven Praedicatien*, 103.
75. Caron, *Seven Praedicatien*, 105.
76. Caron, *Seven Praedicatien*, 105.
77. Heidelberg Catechism, question and answer 128.
78. Caron, *De Wegh Na den Hemel*, question and answer 44, 31.

5

Transfer of Reformed Religious Concepts in the East Indies

Administrations of the Sacraments and Their Complexities

To BEGIN LOOKING AT the complexities of the transplantation of Reformed worship in the East Indies, we will first look at the practice and teaching of baptism administered by the Reformed ministers in the archipelago. In the newly established Reformed churches in the East Indies baptism became one of the most important theological teachings and ecclesial practices. When the ministers brought people—adults as well as infants—into baptism in the Reformed tradition, they had to make sure that the people understood the meaning of baptism the way it was explained in the Reformed faith. It was important for the ministers to emphasize the Calvinistic doctrine and practice of baptism, because the Roman Catholics had baptized people following their theology and practices. At the same time, the Reformed ministers had to be able to explain the meaning of baptism in the language that the people understood. This means that they had to borrow concepts and terminology that were already present in the lives and experience of the indigenous people. In so doing, some creative efforts emerged, and these efforts enhanced and enriched the spread of Christianity in the East Indies. Particularly helpful for modern readers to look at how baptism was administered are Danckaerts' translation of the Heidelberg Catechism and his translation of forms of baptism for infants and also for adults (*Formulier om den Heiligen Doop aan de kinderen te bedienen* and *Formulier om den Heiligen*

Doop aan de volwassenen te bedienen), which were the standard forms of baptism in the Netherlands were then transported to the East Indies. Danckaerts included these forms for baptism at the end of his translation of the Heidelberg Catechism.

Within Reformed Protestantism, baptism is explained as the sign of God's covenant that is sealed to the children of believers. As previously mentioned in chapter 1, the ecclesial practices of Dutch Reformed church were governed by the church order of the Synod of Dordt. In the East Indies, the church order of Batavia became the authoritative document to govern worship in the Indies.[1] The two church orders insisted that baptism should be administered as soon as the baby was born, in the public assembly when the word of God was preached. The church order of Batavia specified that these public assemblies were the ones celebrated on Sunday or Thursday mornings, whereas Dordt's church order did not mention baptism on a midweek worship service.[2] In Batavia, baptism on Thursday morning was mostly intended for babies who were born weak during the week. Here we see that the flexibility to allow baptism during Thursday morning worship was also intended to ensure that there would still be a sermon delivered when the baptism occurred.

In rural areas where there were not many church services, baptism could be administered privately on any day of the week. One main requirement still remained, namely that a sermon must be said at baptism. In the Batavia church order the ministers were reminded that even in the case of emergency baptism they should still preach a short sermon or a homily in order to avoid superstition.[3] This particular article in the church order was an indication of a fight against Roman Catholicism that was brought by Portuguese before the Dutch came. Carrying the medieval practice into the seventeenth century, the Roman Catholics allowed midwives to baptize in case of emergency.

In the Malay translation of the Heidelberg Catechism Danckaerts communicated the covenantal nature of baptism to the indigenous people by using the word *cawoul* in question and answer 74 of the catechism.[4] This word is originally an Arabic word that signifies a solemn vow. In the

1. DKO, article 56; and BKO 1643, article 45.
2. BKO 1624, article 22; BKO 1643, article 45.
3. BKO 1624, article 22; BKO 1643, article 45.
4. Heidelberg Catechism, question and answer 74, in Danckaerts, *Cetechismus attau Adjaran derri agamma Christaon*, 32.

Malay-Dutch dictionary that Danckaerts and Wiltens developed in 1623, this word was listed as the synonym for the Dutch word *verbond*.[5] This Arabic word, which had become a loan word that was widely used in the religious context by the Muslim people, was the choice to translate the biblical concept of covenant. This is a demonstration how the transplantation of a Christian concept was done using a word or concept that was familiar to the people. At the same time, this also shows that assimilation of concepts and language occurs every time two cultures interact with each other.

The term "baptism" was translated using the already available Portuguese word *bautismo* as well as the word *mandi*. In the translation of the catechism Danckaerts interchanged between the two words. This seems to be a simple step that Danckaerts took in order to ensure that the people understood the meaning of baptism. The people had seen Roman Catholic baptism before. When the Heidelberg Catechism was translated into Malay in 1623 the sacrament of baptism had been administered numerous times by the Jesuits, and therefore Danckaerts could easily use the Portuguese term *bautismo* to refer to baptism. To instill the Reformed concept of baptism as the washing away of sins, Danckaerts employed the Malay word *mandi* in questions and answers 69–71.[6] This word literally means "to take a bath" and the use of this word to signify the washing away of sins in baptism was perfect. Just as the people knew that taking a bath removes dirt from the body, baptism washes away the spiritual impurity. The use of the word *mandi* carried the most suitable connotation to show the removal of all dirt and impurities. The interplay between the foreign, religiously charged word *bautismo* and the common, regularly used word *mandi* made the communication of the concept of baptism to the people solid, so that they could understand the concept well.

The term "rebirth" or *wedergeboorte* in question 73 of the Heidelberg Catechism was translated as *manusia barou*, "a new person," in the Malay edition of the catechism.[7] It seems that Danckaerts tried to avoid the complicated theological concept of rebirth or regeneration. The idea of becoming a new person in Christ is certainly a biblical concept. It was probably easier for the indigenous people to grasp the idea of becoming a new person rather than understanding how rebirth could happen.

---

5. Wiltens and Danckaerts, *Kitab Bacattahan daulo Malaio commedien Holando*, 81.
6. Danckaerts, *Catechismus*, 30.
7. Danckaerts, *Catechismus*, 33.

Transfer of Reformed Religious Concepts in the East Indies

In *De Wegh na den Hemel*, Franchois Caron translated "baptism" as *mandian sakti*.[8] As in the translation of the Heidelberg Catechism, the word *mandi* or *mandian* was commonly used to explain the concept of washing away of sin in baptism. The employment of the word *sakti*, however, is very interesting. In the sermon on the Apostles' Creed, Caron used this word to show the holiness that the Holy Spirit gives to the justified people of God. In Malay, the word is used to refer to somebody or something that possesses a supernatural power. A person who is called *sakti* is believed to own special ability that is both beyond the natural human power and usually comes as the result of the person's efforts in meditation and other spiritual exercises to reach to the divine realm and power. This choice of word in translating the concept of holy baptism in the Reformed faith deserves our attention. In the minds of the indigenous people, becoming a *sakti* person required years of practice and self-discipline in trying to attain some super power from the divine. In the Reformed faith, baptism is called *sakti* to show that salvation comes from God and is not based on human merit. Caron clearly explained the meaning of sacrament from within the Calvinistic theology as *tanda adil daan tsap deri fermang Allah*, or the sign and seal, of the Word of God in Christ.[9] *De Wegh na den Hemel* also marked the fact that Caron worked mainly in the Moluccas Islands. He consistently used the word *beta* for first-person singular nominative case "I" in this catechism.[10] The word *beta* is uniquely used by the Moluccans, and not normally used by other ethnic groups in the East Indies. This use indicates that Caron wrote the small catechism mainly for the use of the Moluccans.

While the main theological teaching in the Malay form of baptism was similar to the Dutch form of baptism expressed in the "Formulier om den Heiligen Doop aan de kinderen te bedienen,"[11] there is a noticeable difference between the Dutch and Malay texts. This difference was due to the contextualization of the rite of baptism to the local situation in the East Indies, as the theological meaning of baptism was kept intact. Both the Dutch and Malay forms of baptism start with the theological explanation of original sin and how sin has separated humans from God. Human beings are not able to save themselves from the wrath of God, and only through

---

8. Caron, *De Wegh na den Hemel*, 22.
9. Caron, *De Wegh na den Hemel*, 22.
10. Caron, *De Wegh na den Hemel*, passim.
11. "Formulier om den Heiligen Doop aan de kinderen te bedienen," in Gereformeerde Kerken in Nederland, *De Formulieren*, 143–47.

the blood of Christ can humans receive salvation. In the Dutch form of baptism this theological teaching is presented by way of an explication, in which the form lays out three theological points to be understood. In summary, the Dutch form states that 1) all humans were born in original sin, 2) baptism washes away our sin through the blood of Christ, and 3) once we are baptized in the name of the Trinity we are called to obey God.[12] In the Malay edition, the form of baptism starts by directly addressing the parents of the child to remind them of the biblical teaching of how sin entered into the world. The form takes time in retelling the story of God's creation with a specific mention of Adam and Eve, and how they were created in righteousness. But then Adam and Eve succumbed to the temptation of Satan and fell into sin.[13] The form then moves on to remind the parents of the child—and thus to all who are present at the baptism—that God so loves the world, and that He provides way of redemption and forgiveness of sin through the blood of Jesus Christ. At the end of this introduction, the form explicitly states that God also loves the little children, and he also provides forgiveness of sin to the little children.[14]

This retelling of the story of the fall and the beginning of original sin and redemption through the blood of Christ was a strategic approach, not just for the theological purpose of reminding the parents of why baptism is necessary, but also to remind the whole congregation witnessing baptism of the core message of the Scripture. By hearing this message every time they witnessed baptism, the congregation would be reminded again of the basic message of the Bible. Thus, the Malay form of baptism achieved the same objectives as that of the Dutch form in reminding the people of the necessity of baptism, but instead of preaching or lecturing to the people, it told the story of sin and redemption.

The Malay edition the form of baptism uses the terms *hati yang betul* and *moumin* to describe the original human condition of "holiness and righteousness" before the Adam's fall into sin. The word *hati* means "heart," and *betul* means "right." The word *moumin* is originally an Arabic word that was used widely among the Islamic community. In the original Arabic, this word was used to describe a person who is religiously upright. In his Malay-Dutch dictionary, Danckaerts used the word *moumin* as the synonym

---

12. "Formulier om den Heiligen Doop," 143–44.

13. "Forme vanden Kinder-doop," in Gereformeerde Kerken in Nederland, *De Formulieren*, 70.

14. "Forme vanden Kinder-doop," 71.

of the Dutch word *heylich*,[15] or "holy" in English. This is another example of contextualization and adaptation of theological concept. As a Reformed minister Danckaerts understood that the original condition of human beings before the fall of Adam was holy and righteous. He adopted the term *moumin* to describe holiness, even though there was a marked distinction between the two concepts. In Islam, being *moumin* means that a person must be obedient and upright in keeping the religious requirements. The emphasis is on the efforts of the person to diligently keep the religious laws. However, because the term was widely used among the people, and the people understood the concept of *moumin* as being upright and righteous, Danckaerts was willing to use the term even to refer to the original human condition before sin entered into the world.

The significance of baptism by water is emphasized in the Malay form of baptism. The symbolic nature of the washing away by water to refer to the washing away of sin by the blood of Christ is closely connected to the belief that baptism is the seal of God's promise. The seal is linked to the covenant between God and human beings.[16] In one short paragraph, the form brings together the distinctively Reformed theology of baptism. Like in the Heidelberg Catechism, the term used for "covenant" in the form of baptism is *cawoul*.[17] As described above, this term also had its origin in the Arabic language and was used by the Islamic people to express a solemn vow to God. The form of baptism used the same term so that the ministers could maintain continuity in the use of terminology. This form also served as a reminder to the people of what they had heard and learned from the catechism.

In a thoroughly Reformed fashion, the form explains that little children still cannot understand the meaning of baptism. But it should not prevent the parents from bringing their children to church be baptized.[18] Unlike the Roman Catholic belief, the form does not say that baptism brings eternal salvation to the infants. Instead, it says that the children will know the teaching of the Bible when they are older, and it is the task of parents and godparents to explain to the children the teaching of the Bible. This explanation is directly followed with the direct question to the father of the child, if he believes that the child was born in sin, and that all sinners must

15. Danckaerts, *Vocabularium*, 27.
16. "Forme vanden Kinder-doop," 72.
17. Danckaerts, *Catechismus*, 32.
18. "Forme vanden Kinder-doop," 73.

be punished by God, and only through the blood of Jesus Christ can the child receive salvation. The father is supposed to answer in the affirmative.[19]

The direct interrogation of just the father in the baptism of children is worth our further attention. This practice is uniquely Reformed in that the father must be present at baptism. According to the church order of Batavia, the ministers must ensure the presence of the father of the baby at baptism.[20] The form of baptism served as the practical application of what the church order required. The interrogation of the father is then followed by the interrogation of the godparents. The minister asks the godparents the same question he asks the father of the baby, to which the godparents must answer in affirmative.[21] The interrogation also included a question to the father and the godparents if they believe that the Protestant religion is the only true religion, and without this true religion people cannot go to heaven.[22] This question places the polemic between Protestantism and other faith traditions, including Roman Catholicism, right at the center of the sacrament of baptism. In this question the central crux of the Reformation lies. The Reformed ministers had to ensure that the people knew that other religions are superstitious. This is especially important considering that Roman Catholicism was already present in the archipelago before Reformed Protestantism came. The Jesuit missionaries baptized babies with the belief that unbaptized babies who died in infancy would not go to heaven. The liturgy of baptism in the Reformed church had to combat that false teaching. It shows that baptism does not bring babies to heaven. However, the Protestant religion, or *Agamma Nasrani* as it was referred to in the seventeenth century, is the true religion. Only through this religion can people come to God and receive eternal salvation. This particular question in the liturgy of baptism summarized the entire battle over true and false religion as it was done in the Reformation era. The liturgy made it clear that it is the true Protestant religion that brought people to salvation, and not just the act of baptism. This was important for the parents of the baby and the entire congregation to hear, as a reminder against the theology of Roman Catholicism, that eternal salvation does not just depend on participation in the sacrament, but it is connected to the whole faith of the Reformed Protestant church.

19. "Forme vanden Kinder-doop," 73.
20. BKO 1624, article 22; BKO 1643, article 45.
21. "Forme vanden Kinder-doop," 74.
22. "Forme vanden Kinder-doop," 74.

In the liturgy of infant baptism, the next set of questions and answers to the father of the child and the godparents is focused on the Christian education of the child. The minister asks the father and the godparents separately, if they are willing to instruct the child, if s/he continues to live, in the teaching of the Protestant religion, exactly as the religion requires.[23] It is clear through the interrogation of the godparents that their function was to replace the parents of the child in providing Christian instruction just in case the parents die young. This part of the liturgy demonstrates the Reformed church's emphasis on the instruction and the teaching of the true religion. The presence of the godparents is needed just for the purpose of securing an uninterrupted Christian instruction and upbringing of the child just in case her parents die when she is still young. This is a noted difference if compared to Roman Catholic baptism, in which the presence of the godparents is to represent the child in the interrogation. The godparents should answer, on behalf of the baptized child, if s/he believes in God, if s/he desires to be baptized, and also in the renunciation of the devil and his powers. Here we see a marked difference between the Reformed and Roman Catholic baptismal liturgy.

In the Dutch liturgy, after the reminder of original sin and the need of salvation in Christ, there is also the explanation of the covenantal character of baptism that is rooted in God's covenant with Abraham. The liturgy explicitly quotes Genesis 17:17 and Peter's sermon in Acts 2:39 to show how baptism of children of believers is the continuity of the Old Testament concept of circumcision. The children of believing parents are included in the covenant between God and his people.[24] Then the liturgy includes the story in Mark 10:16 where Jesus brought little children to him to show that he cares for them too. This section is then followed by a prayer of invocation that includes the reminder of God's saving work to Noah and his family and deliverance of Israel from Pharaoh's hands through the Red Sea, which symbolized baptism. The prayer ends with thanksgiving for God's great gift of salvation through his son Jesus Christ.[25] The prayer is then followed by a direct address to the parents and also the godparents. However, the liturgy does not explicitly use the term "godparents." Instead, it calls them *die mede ten Doop komen*,[26] or "those who come to the baptism." While the liturgy

23. "Forme vanden Kinder-doop," 74.
24. "Formulier om den Heiligen Doop," 144.
25. "Formulier om den Heiligen Doop," 145.
26. "Formulier om den Heiligen Doop," 145.

does not explicitly use the term "godparents," it is clear from the context and content of this section of the liturgy that "those who come to the baptism" refers to godparents. This part of the liturgy is basically an interrogation of the parents and the godparents that summarizes their belief that their child was born in sin, is in need of salvation that comes only through Jesus Christ, and their promise to teach and instruct the child in faith.[27]

The Dutch liturgy clearly specifies the content of Christian faith education that the parents and godparents must give the child, namely that they must teach her the Old and the New Testament, the Apostles' Creed, and the belief of the church. The Malay liturgy, however, does not include this detail. This is due to the fact that the indigenous people of the East Indies did not yet have a direct access to the entire Scripture. In both the Dutch and Malay forms the interrogation is directly followed by baptism in the name of God the Father, the Son and the Holy Spirit. Compared to other liturgies of baptism of other Reformed traditions in Europe, the liturgy of baptism in the Dutch Reformed churches in the East Indies is much simpler. There is no renunciation of the devil and his powers, and there is no prayer for the water of baptism. This liturgy follows the pattern of the liturgy of baptism of the Reformed church in the Netherlands.[28] In the Malay liturgy, however, we find the translation of the Trinitarian name of God was taken from Portuguese words, coupled with Malay words. This is consistent with what we see in the Malay translation of the Heidelberg Catechism that we already discussed above. The name of "God the Father" is translated using the Portuguese word *Deos* for God and the Malay word *Bapa* meaning "father." The name "God the Son" was translated as *Deos Anac*, with the word *anak* as the Malay word for "son" and the name "Holy Spirit" was translated as *Spirito Santo*, a purely Portuguese term. Here we see that the influence of the Roman Catholic culture and the Portuguese language in the Reformed Protestant church in the East Indies. Such influence was understandable, considering that the indigenous people were already exposed to the Portuguese language and Roman Catholicism before the arrival of the Dutch. When the Reformed theology and ecclesiastical practices were introduced to the people, it was very logical that the Dutch ministers used elements of religious practices that were readily available to the indigenous people.

27. "Formulier om den Heiligen Doop," 146.
28. "Formulier om den Heiligen Doop," 146.

Transfer of Reformed Religious Concepts in the East Indies

Both liturgies end with a prayer. The prayer in the Malay liturgy was a close translation of the prayer in the Dutch Reformed church's liturgy of baptism. In the prayer the minister starts with an expression of gratitude to God the Almighty who has granted pardon from sin, for the people, and also for their children, through the blood of Jesus Christ.[29] This opening line of the prayer stands right at the center of Reformed theology. It reminds the people that pardon of sin and eternal salvation are the gift of God. Salvation is not something that humans can achieve. And because this is a gift, humans are called to offer gratitude to God for his gift. Moreover, the gift of salvation is also available to the children of believers, who receive salvation through the same way, namely through the blood of Jesus Christ.

The Reformed theology of covenant in baptism is expressed in the next part of the prayer. Like in the Heidelberg Catechism and in the explanation of the nature of baptism mentioned in the liturgy, the prayer calls baptism the sign and seal. In Malay it is called ... *seperti dengan tanda lagi dengan tsjap satou* ...[30] The word *tsjap* in Malay can either mean the branding mark on a cattle or a signet ring that kings used to seal a document and thus to ensure its authenticity. Either way the term provides a good and clear image that baptism is a sign and seal given by God to assure his promise of salvation.

The conviction of assurance of salvation is expressed through the thanksgiving statement that God has made the baptized child a "new person," *manusia barou*, and a petition that God keeps his promise to the child. This part of prayer is important to show the people that baptism is concerned with the making of the new person out of the child. She was born in sin, but she has received the grace of redemption in Christ through baptism. Here is where the theology of justification finds its practical expression. It is God who has completed the work of justification for the baptized child. God has made the child a new person, a justified person who has been pardoned from her sins. Afterwards the prayer follows with a request of sanctification. The minister asks God the Holy Spirit to lead and guide the child, when he grows up, that he may be obedient to God, worship God and follow God until the day he dies. In the Malay liturgy the prayer ends with the Lord's Prayer. The Dutch liturgy, however, does not include the Lord's Prayer in the prayer after baptism.[31]

29. "Formulier om den Heiligen Doop," 146; and "Forme vanden Kinder-doop," 75.
30. Forme vanden Kinder-doop, 75.
31. "Forme vanden Kinder-doop," 75; and "Formulier om den Heiligen Doop aan de

The Way to Heaven

In its practice, the newly established Reformed church in the East Indies faced various challenging issues with regard to infant baptism. The first issue that appeared was the question of the baptism of children born of Asian women and European men. Many of these women were slaves and the babies were illegitimate. In some cases the fathers of the babies were no longer around, or those men never acknowledged that the babies were theirs. Reformed baptism, following the practice of Calvin's Geneva, required that the father be present at the time of baptism. This requirement guaranteed that the father would support the baby and that the baby was legitimate. The absence of the fathers and the legitimacy of the babies raised difficult issue for the Dutch ministers. The ministers, according to Dubbeldam, were pressed by this dilemma: baptizing the babies meant that the church allowed or even accepted the sin that caused the babies to be born, but not baptizing the babies denied the sacrament.[32] Theologically, baptism is about God's grace and therefore should be administered to the babies. However, the question of the sin of the parents still lingered. The church council in Amsterdam on March 21, 1611, wrestled with the question and decided that in such cases, if at least one parent was a believer, the church should administer baptism to the child. But then, the council also declared that the church should make a distinction between the baptisms of legitimate children from that of illegitimate ones.[33]

From Batavia Hulsebos asked a similar question to Amsterdam. On March 29, 1618, he wrote a letter to the council, asking whether children of the slaves that were accepted into Christian families and illegitimate children should be baptized.[34] Hulsebos' question was considered very difficult to decide. As the issue arose right at the time that the National Synod of Dordrecht was happening, the church council decided to bring the issue to the the National Synod.[35] Schutte suspects that the National Synod of Dordt was not very knowledgeable of the issue that Hulsebos had to face in Batavia, and that Hulsebos' question could be interpreted different ways.[36] The question regarding the baptism of European fathers and Asian women

kinderen te bedienen," 147.

32. Dubbeldam, *De Gereformeerde Kerken in Nederland en de Zending in Oost-Indie*, 35.

33. Dubbeldam, *De Gereformeerde Kerken*, 36.

34. Dubbeldam, *De Gereformeerde Kerken*, 36.

35. Dubbeldam, *De Gereformeerde Kerken*, 37.

36. Schutte, "Between Amsterdam and Batavia," 35.

Transfer of Reformed Religious Concepts in the East Indies

was easier to answer. The National Synod agreed to allow baptism of such children, because such baptism fell under the larger agreement with the baptismal policy of the Reformed church in the Netherlands. The issue was discussed at the seventeenth session of the National Synod on November 30, 1618.[37] Because the issue was raised at the very end of the session, the synod decided to continue looking at the matter again during the nineteenth session that was held on Monday, December 3, 1618.[38]

At the nineteenth session the synod decided that adults who were able to make their own decision should be baptized, even if their parents objected to their baptisms. But the synod was divided regarding the baptism of children of slaves. The delegates from England, Hesse, Bremen, Zeeland and Friesland, as well as the Dutch professors thought that these children should be baptized so that they would be included in the household of Christ. These delegates appealed to the Abrahamic covenant in which every male member of Abraham's household, including his slaves and the children of the slaves, was circumcised. These delegates also used Paul's decision to baptize all the members of the household of the jailer in Philippi as their foundation that children of the slaves in the Indies should also be baptized.[39] The majority of the people at the synod, however, disagreed. These majority of the people argued that the slaves were not part of the covenantal family of God, and therefore their children were not members of the covenantal family. The president of the synod did not want to take a vote on the issue and suggested that the delegates think further on the matter.[40]

The reality in Batavia and other parts of the East Indies revealed that children of the slaves were baptized based on the argument of adoption into the covenantal family, the church. Dubbeldam reported that the majority of the children being baptized in this manner were the illegitimate children of Asian slaves from European fathers.[41] The church in Batavia, according to Schutte, saw the baptisms of these children as very important to the Christian community, and the church ordered that all children be baptized,

---

37. Brandt, *History of the Reformation*, vol. 3, bk. 33, p. 34.

38. For more elaborate discussion on the Synod of Dordt on the issue of the baptism of children of slaves in the East Indies, see Kajajan, *De Pro-Acta der Dordtsche Synode in 1618*.

39. Brandt, *History of the Reformation*, vol. 3, bk. 33, p. 35.

40. Brandt, *History of the Reformation*, vol. 3, bk. 33, p. 35.

41. Debbeldam, *De Gereformeerde Kerken*, 215.

even children born out of wedlock. The parents would then be required to be married, and if they refused they would be placed under church discipline.⁴² And as Schutte recognizes, after the Synod of Dordt was over, in the Moluccas the position of the minority group at the Synod of Dordt was applied. The ministers regularly baptized the children of the Muslims, as long as Christian education could be required.⁴³

On June 4, 1618, Danckaerts wrote a letter to Hulsebos, outlining his view of baptism of children of the slaves. Danckaerts said that if at least one parent of the child was Christian, he would baptize the baby. He also acknowledged that the children of unbelieveing parents had been presented to him to be baptized.⁴⁴ Danckaerts' letter provided us with the actual situation that the ministers in the Indies—in the case Ambon—had to face. The situation that Danckaerts and Wiltens saw in Ambon was confirmed by Johannes de Praet, another minister in Ambon,⁴⁵ who wrote to the Heeren XVII on September 5, 1625, to testify that the two ministers had baptized between nine hundred and one thousand people living around the castle in Ambon. De Praet emphasized that the baptisms done by the Dutch ministers were not like the papistic baptisms done by the Portuguese. The adults who were baptized should have enough knowledge of teaching of the Christian faith before they were admitted to baptism.⁴⁶ The church in Ambon ensured that sufficient instruction in Christian belief should be given to the adults before they were baptized, and sufficient instruction should be given to parents who wanted to baptize their children, by way of producing acta that governed church worship.⁴⁷

In most of the catechism books and other literature published in the later years of the seventeenth century, the Lord's Supper was consistently translated into Malay as *Djumahan Petang*.⁴⁸ This term was a literal transla-

42. Schutte, "Between Amsterdam and Batavia," 36.

43. Schutte, "Between Amsterdam and Batavia," 37.

44. ANRI, Archief protestantse gemeenten 136, fol. 1–4.

45. De Praet came to Ambon as a minister in September 1624 and stayed there until his death in 1633. He worked with Danckaerts closely as he was in Ambon. Bruijn, *Biographisch Woordenboek*, 348.

46. NA, VOC 1084, fol. 214r.

47. "Acten des kerckenraets der gemeynte van Amboyna sindt de maent september anno

1625," in Manuscripts, ANRI, Archief protestantse gemeenten 212, fol. 103–110, especially acta 4 and 9.

48. See, for instance, Sebastian Danckaerts' Malay translation of the Heidelberg

Transfer of Reformed Religious Concepts in the East Indies

tion of the Dutch word for the sacrament, *avondmaal*, literally "evening meal." The word *djumahan* in Malay was the translation of *maal*, and *petang* was the translation of *avont*, "evening."[49] The 1611 edition of the *Sovrat ABC* translated the Lord's Supper as *djamoe Christy*,[50] or "the feast of Christ," perhaps because this small catechism book was the very first one to be translated into Malay. At such an early stage of the presence of the VOC and Reformed Protestantism in the archipelago, the concept of the Lord's Supper as the feast that Jesus Christ prepared for his people was probably easier to communicate to the Malay-speaking people. The term has stronger theological message to show that when the people partake in the sacrament they come to the feast that Christ has prepared for them. The later translation of the sacrament as *djumahan petang* brought the concept to be more in line with the practice and terminology of the Dutch Reformed church but the sacredness of the sacrament was a little lost in the term.

While the Reformed church in the East Indies accepted both infants and adults to be baptized, the church was very strict in admitting adults to partake in the Lord's Supper. Following the common practice of the Reformed churches in Europe, the church in the Indies imposed on the need for the people to understand the significant doctrinal teachings of the church and also to have upright moral conduct as Christians. Because the church in the Indies wanted to make sure that people who partook in the sacrament were really worthy of it, the church practiced what was called the *sacramentsscheiding*, or "separated sacraments."[51] What happened there was that new converts into Christianity who had been baptized as adults were not automatically allowed to partake in the Lord's Supper. They were only allowed to take the Supper after a certain trial period.

The practice of separating the sacraments was in many ways unorthodox. The new converts of the East Indies were already received as Christians and were allowed to worship together with the rest of the congregation. They were allowed to be married at church and when they had children the church also baptized their children. And yet the church denied them the sacrament. While it is understandable that Christians should examine

---

Catechism, *Catechismus attau Adjaran derri Agamma Christaon*, questions and answers 75–82 and passim; and Caron's *De Wegh na den Hemel*, questions and answers 31–34.

49. Danckaerts and Wiltens, *Vocabularium*, 5.

50. Ruyl, *Sovrat ABC*, A5 recto.

51. Dubbeldam, *De Gereformeerde Kerken*, 184; Schutte, "Between Amsterdam and Jakarta," 34.

themselves before they come to the Lord's Supper, the prohibition to partake in the Lord's Supper was certainly a demonstration of some legalistic approach toward Christianity. In the time when the Dutch were starting to get their grips over the land and the people of the East Indies, the separation of the sacraments seemed to be a part of the VOC's effort to control the people. The people had to obey whatever the authority told them to do. Within the scope of the church, the power was translated into the prohibition for adults to take Communion. As Schutte has pointed out, it is doubtful that this prohibition was motivated by the church's concerns for the people's eternal salvation.[52]

Niemeijer says that in the Netherlands the classis Walcheren was against the practice, and in 1648 one wrote from the classis that the separation of the sacraments was against the teaching of the Reformed church and against the nature of baptism. The classis emphasized that this practice should no longer be continued.[53] Niemeijer further noted that upon receiving the note from Walcheren the church in Ambon made some modification, allowing the pastors to make some "alteration" to allow people to partake in the Supper.[54] The minister in Batavia did not really like the pressure that came from the Netherlands, particularly the one coming from the classis Walcheren. The ministers recognized that more instruction was badly needed for adults who wanted to be baptized.[55] They made promises that they would provide more instruction to the candidates for baptism so that when these people were finally baptized, they would also be ready to partake in the Lord's Supper. The decision of the ministers in Batavia seems to be a more appropriate step in the remedy of the issue of the separation of the sacraments. Instead of denying baptized people the right to celebrate Communion, the church should make greater efforts to prepare candidates for baptism more intensively, so that when they were finally baptized, they already had sufficient knowledge of their faith and the right conducts as Christians. Despite the fact that the church put so much restriction demands for people to be baptized, and from the outside the restrictions may sound prohibitive for people to become Christians, church membership continued to increase.[56]

---

52. Schutte, "Between Amsterdam and Jakarta," 34.
53. Niemeijer, *Calvinisme en Coloniale Stadscultuur*, 173.
54. Niemeijer, *Calvinisme en Coloniale Stadscultuur*, 173.
55. Niemeijer, *Calvinisme en Coloniale Stadscultuur*, 174.
56. Schutte, "Between Amsterdam and Batavia," 34.

Some Measure of Progress on the Establishment of Reformed Protestantism in the First Century of the VOC

Emphasis on providing knowledge of the basic teachings of Christianity had always been in the foreground of the works of the Dutch ministers among the natives of the East Indies. As evidenced through the publications of several catechetical materials and sermons in Malay, the ministers wanted to establish Christian churches and communities who understood what they believed. Adults who wanted to be baptized had to be able to express their beliefs. Clear evidence of serious effort to measure people's knowledge of basic Christian doctrines could be seen through the report of Wouter Melchiorsz and Jeuriaen Pietersz of the conversion of some people in Rozengain in 1622.[57]

In August of 1622 Melchiorsz and Petersz met with several *orangcayas*, or local leaders of the community, and talked about their Christian belief. Woutersz talked with them and asked them questions regarding their belief in God the Father, the Creator of heaven and earth, creation and fall of human beings in Adam and Eve and redemption of sinful human beings in Jesus Christ.[58] The people indicated some knowledge of these basic beliefs of Christianity and that they were willing to support education for the young people. From the visitation Woutersz got the impression that the people understood the significance of following the law of God. Woutersz' two-week visitation trip was focused on talking to people and asking questions of how much they could express their knowledge of Christianity. This effort demonstrates the general emphasis of the church to make sure that these new Christians knew what they believed. This emphasis was in accordance with the general practice of the Reformed churches in Europe. Ever since the Reformation in the sixteenth century, the Calvinist branch of Protestantism always wanted to make sure that Christians could express their doctrinal knowledge. Faith for the Reformed churches must be an informed faith, not some kind of blind adherence to whatever the church teaches them. In the East Indies we see how similar approach to Christianity was implanted and applied.

---

57. See, "Verslag Betreffende de Bekering van Rozengain door DS W. Melchiorsz. en Vrijburger Jeuriaen
    Pietersz, Banda Neira, 31 Augustus 1622," in Stadsarchief Amsterdam 379, Archief Classis Amsterdam, 184, fol. 46–56.2

58. Stadsarchief Amsterdam 379, Archief Classis Amsterdam, 184, fol. 46.

The Way to Heaven

The number of children being baptized in the castle of Ambon and the neighboring villages was impressive. Between 1625 and 1631 there were 1,297 children baptized, with the following breakdown: 32 in the year 1625, 432 in 1626, 225 in 1627, 125 in the year 1628, 246 in the year 1629, 215 in 1630 and 22 in 1631.[59] Beyond the castle of Ambon, large number of baptisms was also performed in various islands. Rogier Hendrickxz baptized 276 between 1628 and 1628, Johan de Praet baptized 162 children of the smaller Amboina islands in 1629, de Praet together with candidate minister Rutenius baptized 267 more children in the more remote islands of Amboina in 1629 and in April of 1630 alone Wouter Melchiorsz baptized 96 children. In total, there were 2226 children being baptized between 1625 and 1631 under the jurisdiction of Ambon alone.[60]

Justus Heurnius reported similar progress in the number of baptized children. Heurnius was a dedicated minister whose work in the East Indies was well appreciated. He first came to the East Indies in 1624, first to Batavia where he preached in Malay. In 1630 he visited several islands to the eastern end of the Indies, including Aru, Kei, Solor and Timor. In 1633 he moved to Amboina where he ministered to the people in Honimoa.[61] In August 1634 Heurnius wrote a long letter to the Amsterdam chamber to explain the work he did in the East Indies. He reported that he visited each village, which was called *negrij*, once every three months, and each time he visited one village he would administer the sacrament of baptism. He said that within a year of his presence in Amboina he had baptized 325 children.[62] Heurnius' report indicates that this was the typical work of an ordained minister who worked in the archipelago. As they visited the villages they also administered the sacraments. The number of children being baptized in just one year was relatively large, and this was an indication that the people in the villages were turning into Protestants and started to gain knowledge of the significance of baptism for their children. In the Ulisian

---

59. Data from "Notitie van de gedoopte kinderen in de eylanden Amboyna t'sedert martii anno 1625 tot
ultimo april anno 1631," manuscript NA, VOC 1102, fol. 368r-v. The manuscript says that there were 1299 children being baptized in Ambon and neighboring vilages, but actual addition of the numbers show that there were only 1297 children being baptized. The descrepancy could have been caused by the fact that some of these numbers in the manuscript were not easily read.

60. Data taken from NA, VOC 1102, fol. 368 recto.

61. Bruijn, *Biographisch Woordenboek*, 180–81.

62. Manuscript, NA, VOC 1113, fol. 826–31.

Transfer of Reformed Religious Concepts in the East Indies

archipelago there were sixteen congregations that Heurnius had to oversee. He worked hard to provide good preaching as well instructions in the Apsotles' Creed, the Lord's Prayer and the Ten Commandments. Realizing that the people did not understand Malay too well, he also worked toward writing the sermons in the language of the Ulisians, as he also translated parts of the Bible, the creed and the prayer into Ulisian. He was insistent that the young people must be instructed in their language, because otherwise they would never understand the basic teaching of Christianity. Further reports of Heurnius illustrate the growth of Protestantism in Ambon well. On September 10, 1636, he wrote a letter to the governor of Ambon, Anthonio van Diemen, to give the Governor detailed report of his ministry. He reported that he just visited the island of Oma and he baptized sixty children there. From Oma he sailed to Aboru where he baptized sixteen children. After that he sailed to Honomoa and baptized eighty-five children. Next he went to Papero, which had four *negerij*, and he baptized fifty children.[63]

The report from the consistory of Ambon regarding the status of the Protestant church and schools written in September 1635 showed that Reformed Christianity grew very fast there. According to the report, baptisms of children and adults happened often. With regard to adult baptism, the report said that people from various backgrounds came to church to be baptized: the Mardijkers of the VOC, the slaves of Dutch people, Japanese, Chinese, as well as natives of Makassar, Malabar and Ceram.[64] The report also stated that many of the adults wanted to be baptized because of their own decision, some because they wanted to be married to Christian spouses, some in order to get better connection with the political power, like what some of the Chinese people did.[65]

In Ambon worship services were done three times each Sunday. At first, in the earlier years of the VOC, the Dutch and Malay services were both conducted together in the morning before noon. But then the people felt that worship service in both languages went too long. They soon decided to separate the two services, with the Dutch service at eight o'clock in the morning, and Malay service at ten o'clock. Later in the day, at two

---

63. Manuscript, NA, VOC 1121, fol. 814–17.

64. Manuscript, NA, VOC 1118, fol. 347 recto–350 verso.

65. The report indicated that some of these Chinese wanted closer relationship with the Dutch and they asked the governor to be their *padrinjo*, or godfather. Manuscript, NA, VOC 1118, fol. 350r.

o'clock, the church had another service in both languages.[66] Further growth and development were reported in the letter sent by the church council in Ambon to the church council of Batavia on September 6, 1643. The church in Ambon communicated to the one in Batavia that after witholding baptism for three or four years, in the fort of Ambon itself there were lately 354 children baptized. In addition, there were 150 children recently baptized in Nusanive, after seven years of no baptism in any *negerij* in that island. There were also 41 children recently baptized in the *negerij* of Hatou.[67] Furthermore, the report said that in Ambon there were two schools—one met at the church building in the fort, and the other met within the quarter of the *Mardijker* (*Mardiekers kwartier*), led by very good school teachers. The report indicated positive growth regarding the status of Christianity in Ambon, because as the number showed, with each child being baptized there would be more children receiving Christian education. The hope certainly was that when these children grew up they would be faithful professing Christians. Later reports from the church council of Ambon continued to show healthy expansion of the church. On September 6, 1644, it was reported that 159 children were baptized at the fort. Men and women were excited to go to church every Sunday, to worship and praise God, the report said. These people came from Islamic backgrounds as well as pagan religions to become Christians. Some came even from as far away as Makassar, Wawani and the island of Buton.[68]

There were areas that did not enjoy continued progress. Only a few years after Heurnius' visitation to the Ulias archipelago there was a sharp decline in Christianity in the archipelago. According to the December 1642 visitation report of Jan Janssen Brundt, there had not been church service or school in session on the islands of Samet, Ulat, Touaha and Papere for quite some time. Brundt strongly thought that this situation needed to be remedied soon. The church council of Ambon wrote to Batavia requesting help to be sent to Ulias.[69] This condition in Ulias was perhaps caused by the remoteness of the island. There was a contrast between Ambon and other islands. It is understandable that Ambon could enjoy fast growth because the city was growing too, and ministers were sent to the city where

---

66. See letter from the consistory of Ambon to Batavia, September 18, 1635, in Manuscript, ANRI, Archief protestantse gemeenten 136, fol. 153.

67. ANRI, Archief protestantse gemeenten 136, fol. 238.

68. ANRI, Archief protestantse gemeenten 136, fol. 246

69. ANRI, Archief protestantse gemeenten 136, fol. 238.

Transfer of Reformed Religious Concepts in the East Indies

they lived and made the city their main dwelling place. Even though the ministers still reached out to the other islands, there was still more work needed to be done on those islands outside of Amboina.

Toward the end of the seventeenth century Petrus van der Vorm[70] wrote a detailed report of the number of school teachers, schools and churches in the Moluccas. The numbers he reported were impressive. In 1692 Van der Vorm showed that in Ambon there were twenty-seven school teachers, twenty schools and nineteen churches. Out of these twenty-seven school teachers, six were the so-called *omlopende leermeesters*, or the itinerant catechism teachers.[71] The works of these itinerant catechism teachers, van der Vorm later explained, included going to the houses of the slaves to teach them from the catechism of St. Aldegonde (or Van Marnix) and the Heidelberg Catechism in Malay, as well as to do the work of the ordinary school teachers.[72] Furthermore, van der Vorm also showed that in the area of Haroekoe there were six school teachers, six schools and six churches. On the island of Liase in Honimoa where Fort Hollandia was located there were eleven school teachers, nine schools and eight churches. On the island of Nusalaut there were six school teachers, six schools and six churches, on the island of Ceram there were eight school teachers, eight schools and eight churches. There were also three small islands that were included in van der Vorm's report, namely the islands of Boanoa, Manipa and Buru, with one school teacher, one school and one church on each island. In total there were sixty-one school teachers, fifty-two schools and fifty churches that van der Vorm saw during his ministry in Ambon.[73]

Van der Vorm noted that the growth of Christianity in the Moluccas was attributable to the use of Malay as the language of instruction at schools. The children were able to understand the language well. At the same time, he also pointed out that the books that were used at school and at church were beneficial for the education to happen. He explicitly mentioned the books he meant one by one, namely the Malay translation of Genesis and the New Testament by Brouwerius, the collection of sermons of Franchois

---

70. Van der Vorm was born in Zeeland in 1664. He came as a preacher in Batavia in 1688. In June 1689 he went to Ambon to minister there, and in 1690 he was stationed in Honimoa. In January 1693 he returned to the Fort of Ambon. He was called by the congregation of Batavia in 1698 where he remained a minister there until his death in 1731. See Bruijn, *Biographisch Woordenboek*, 462.

71. ANRI, Archief protestantse gemeenten 136, no folio number.

72. ANRI, Archief protestantse gemeenten 136, no folio number, point 3.

73. ANRI, Archief protestantse gemeenten 136, no folio number.

Caron and Caspar Wiltens, the *Sourat ABC*, and the small catechism book of St. Aldegonde, *Djalang ca Surga*, as well as the Malay translation of the Heidelberg Catechism, which also included all the forms for baptism, Communion, and the prayers. In addition he also indicated that the Dutch-Malay dictionary, together with the Psalm books, has helped him to advance the spread of the teaching of Christianity in the Moluccas.[74] While appreciating the good result that came out of these works in Malay, van Der Vorm also highlighted the fact that Malay was not the mother tongue of most of the people in Ambon. There were several languages being spoken in the archipelago, and he thought that the church and the VOC had to think further regarding the use of other languages that were the mother tongues of many of the native tribes of the Moluccas. He insisted that in order to bring the gospel and the Reformed faith to these native Ambonese, the message of the gospel must also be delivered in the languages in which the people were most comfortable speaking.

In the rural churches school teachers led worship services. Van der Vorm summarized the liturgy of the worship as follows: the school teacher would start by reading a passage from the New Testament translated by Brouwerius, and then he would read the Ten Commandments or the Apostles' Creed, followed by the singing of some psalms. After the singing there would be congregational prayer. The reading of one of Caron's sermons took the place of preaching in the rural churches. The whole service would then be ended with a prayer for after the sermon.[75]

Following the regulation already laid out in the church order of Batavia in 1643,[76] schools were in session for four days during the week in both mornings and afternoons, on Mondays, Tuesdays, Thursdays and Fridays, and two days a week only in the morning, on Wednesdays and Saturdays. On the afternoons of Wednesdays and Saturdays the children would then have the time to play, just as the church order prescribed.[77] At schools, van der Vorm explained, there were three ranks of pupils. The first rank learned the ABC[78] and the prayers; the second rank studied the catechism of St.

---

74. Manuscript ANRI, Archief protestantse gemeenten 136, no folio number.

75. ANRI, Archief protestantse gemeenten 136, no folio number. See point 3 of van der Vorm's report.

76. BKO 1643, article 79.

77. ANRI, Archief protestantse gemeenten 136, no folio number.

78. Van der Vorm might have meant that the school children read or studied from the *Sovrat ABC*, but he did not explicitly specify whether the children only learned their alphabets or they actually read from the *Sovrat ABC*.

Transfer of Reformed Religious Concepts in the East Indies

Aldegonde,[79] and the third rank learned the Heidelberg Catechism as well as writing and singing.[80] The emphasis on Christian education was one that the church inherited from the Calvinist tradition. As Niemeijer points out, school teachers were very central in carrying out the task or religious education in the Dutch Republic.[81] In the Indies, the school teachers also had similar significance. Niemeijer also shows that in some parts of the East Indies, school teachers were raised from among the indigenous people. In Ternate, for instance, Niemeijer notices the success of the works of indigenous school teachers, who successfully carried out the mission work in the area, as well as teaching in the village schools, performing some church administration works, reading sermons during Sunday worship services and playing the drums during the weekdays to call people to morning and evening prayers.[82]

Van der Vorm's detailed report on the books that were being used at schools and in the churches helps us see how much these materials had been influencial in the establishment of Reformed Protestantism in the East Indies. As we have seen throughout this book these materials were foundational in laying out the basic principles of Christianity to the people. By reading his report we can see that these literatures were actually being used by the school teachers to provide instruction for the children. Therefore, the circulated sermons and catechetical materials we have studied in this book were real tools that were useful to build Reformed Protestantism in the East Indies. These materials became especially important at schools, where the Dutch educated the young people of the East Indies with the hope that when they grew older they would become faithful followers and defenders of the Reformed church.

---

79. Here van der Vorm might have meant the small catechism, *Djalang ca Surga*, or *De Wegh na den Hemel*, because he already mentioned the same catechetical book earlier in his report.

80. ANRI, Archief protestantse gemeenten 136, no folio number.

81. Niemeijer, "Political Rivalry and Early Dutch Reformed Missions," 46.

82. Niemeijer, "Political Rivalry and Early Dutch Reformed Missions," 47.

Conclusion

As this study has demonstrated, the transplantation of the theology and ecclesial practices of the Reformed church in the East Indies in the seventeenth century closely followed the teaching and practice of the Reformed church in the Netherlands, while at the same time also reflected contextualization and adaptation to the situation and condition specific to the people in the East Indies. At the time when the VOC was establishing its grip on the archipelago, the Reformed Protestantism that the Dutch brought attracted a certain group within the population of the East Indies who had direct contacts with the Dutch. The ministers who were sent to the archipelago to provide ministerial service to the Dutch people living in the archipelago soon found themselves spreading the teaching and beliefs of Calvinism to the rest of the inhabitants of the archipelago. The Reformed church grew steadily during the first century of the presence of the Dutch in the region. In following the practices of the Reformed churches in Europe these ministers saw that education was an important step in bringing people into the Reformed faith. In the sixteenth-century Reformation era education was meant to turn young people away from the medieval theology and practices those of the Reformation. In the seventeenth-century East Indies education was to turn away the youth—the future generation of the people—from Roman Catholicism, Islam and pagan religions into the beliefs of the Reformed church. Catechisms were the most important tools to educate these young people. The production of several catechisms in Malay served the purpose of providing the young people in the East Indies with texts to study how to read and write as well as fundamental Reformed doctrines.

Closely connected to education at schools was education of the people at church by way of sermons. These sermons reinforced the content of the

Conclusion

Reformed faith that the people learned through school and through the constant teachings of the ministers and other church workers, the school teachers and the comforters of the sick. As these church workers read and reread the collection of sermons written by ordained ministers, they spread the teachings of the Reformed church deeper and deeper into the remote areas of the archipelago. Besides functioning as teaching tool for the new Christians, these sermons also functioned as a polemical tool against Islam, paganism and Roman Catholicism. Most of these sermons were polemical on the issue of the true religion that would bring people to heaven. Many of the sermons studied in this book openly attack the beliefs of pagan religions, Islam and Roman Catholicism. The Islamic people always had the greatest longing for heaven but they never had the assurance. The Roman Catholics emphasized the sacraments, especially baptism, as the way to heaven. However, the sermons demonstrated that neither was the assurance for eternal life in heaven. They showed that knowledge of the true God, relationship between God and human beings, understanding of the seriousness of the fall and redemption in Christ in the form of justification and sanctification were the answer. Thus, these sermons showed emphasis in theological knowledge. This emphasis had become the characteristic of the Reformed faith all along. The Dutch ministers who transplanted this knowledge to the indigenous people in the East Indies only repeated what they inherited from their predecessors, and this became the strong foundation for their works in the new land.

The presentation of the teaching and the practices of the Reformed church in the East Indies did not happen in a vacuum. The presence of Roman Catholicism in the archipelago functioned as a point of reference against which the Reformed ministers had to fight, but also from which they could learn. The translations of several terms pertaining to Christian theology and church practices employed words and terms that were originally from the Portuguese language and widely used in the Roman Catholic Church because those words were already available in the daily experience of the people. This is an example of the adaptation and accommodation that happened as the Reformed church transplanted its teachings in the new land.

The communication of the Reformed views and theology involved the fight against Islam as well as utilization of Islamic concepts to explain certain religious concepts in Reformed Protestantism. In the East Indies, the Reformed church's insistence that Reformed Protestantism is the only true religion was expressed in the catechisms and the sermons. Islam, however, also provided some assistance to the Reformed church in the East Indies. The employment of certain Arabic words in the catechisms and sermons showed that the Reformed faith could not stand alone when it underwent a process of transplantation in the East Indies. While still deeply rooted in the teachings of the sixteenth-century Reformation, the Reformed faith also owed to other religions, cultures and languages in order that it could be clearly communicated to the indigenous people, and in order for the people to understand the content being communicated to them.

The sermons of Wiltens, Danckaerts and Caron followed a similar approach to that of the sixteenth-century Reformation. In line with the belief of the Reformed churches in Europe, they emphasized the people's knowledge of the Lord's Prayer, the Ten Commandments and the Apostles' Creed as the most fundamental knowledge for their faith. Their sermons were reflections of their adherence to the Reformed tradition. At the same time, especially when the sermons touched on the area of polemics against Roman Catholicism or paganism, they also reflected some indications of propaganda. The propaganda was meant to show that first of all the Reformed teaching is superior to all other teachings, if not the best. And because they represented the Dutch people and government, over against their enemy the Portuguese, they also demonstrated in their sermons the superiority of the Dutch.

The works of these ministers in producing catechisms and sermons could also be seen as their way of doing missions. Even though they were not missionaries in the modern sense of the word, they brought Christianity to the indigenous people of the East Indies. As this book has revealed, by looking at the production of catechisms and sermons in Malay these ministers further spread the gospel into the foreign land. They spread the gospel first and foremost by the transfer of religious knowledge, doctrine and practice. As true children of the Reformation of the sixteenth century, they emphasized that knowledge of the content of Christianity should be the foundation for their faith. The productions of the catechisms and sermons preceded the translations of the Bible into Malay. This further illustrates the ministers' approach to missions. They saw that the people as the recipients of the Gospel message should start with strong foundation in the teachings of the church. The catechisms and sermons presented the Bible indirectly to the people. However, if they closely followed the teachings of the church communicated through these sermons and catechisms, they would end up with a good knowledge of the Bible too, even before the Bible had been fully translated into the language that they could understand.

Bibliography

Adjaran dalam Jang Manna Jadi Caberadjar Capalla Capallanja derri Agamma Christaon. Amsterdam: Paulus Matthysz, 1682.
Aritonang, Jan Sihar, and Karel Steenbrink, editors. *A History of Christianity in Indonesia.* Leiden: Brill, 2008.
Bartoli, D., and J. P. Maffei. *The Life of St. Francis Xavier, Apostle of the Indies and Japan.* New York: P. O'Shea, 1889.
Bast, Robert J. *Honor Your Fathers: Catechisms and the Emergence of a Patriarchal Ideology in Germany 1400-1600.* Leiden: Brill, 1997.
Blussé, Leonard. *Strange Company: Chinese Settlers, Mestizo Women and the Dutch in VOC Batavia.* Dordrecht-Holland: Foris, 1986.
Boxer, C. R., editor. *A True Description of the Mighty Kingdoms of Japan and Siam 1663.* London: Argonaut, 1935.
Brandt, Gerard. *The History of the Reformation and Other Ecclesiastical Transactions in and about the Low-Countries.* Vol. 3. London: T. Wood, 1722.
Bruijn, C. A. L. van Troostenburg de. *Biographisch Woordenboek van Oost-Indische Predikanten.* Nijmegen: P. J. Milborn, 1893.
———. *De Hervormde Kerk in Nederlandsch Oost-Indie onder de Oost-Indische Compagnie (1602-1795).* Arnheim: H. A. Tjeenk Willink, 1884.
Calvin, John. *Institutes of the Christian Religion.* Edited by John T. McNeill, translated by Ford Lewis Battles. 2 vols. Philadelphia: Westminster, 1960.
Caron, Franchois Jr. *Voorbeeldt des openbaeren Godtsdienst bestaende in de verhandelinge van de XII articulen des geloofs, de Wet Godes, 't gebed des Heeren, mitsgaders de feets, bid en dank-texten te dienste der Inlandste Christenen op Amboine in 40 predicaetien eenvoudelyck gestalt.* Amsterdam: Paulus Matheys, 1693.
———. *De Wegh na den Hemel, Aengewesen in een kleyn vraegh-boeksken* Amsterdam: Paulus Matthys, n.d.
Coleridge, Henry James. *The Life and Letters of St. Francis Xavier.* Vol. 2. London: Burns and Oates, 1876.
Danckaerts, Sebastian. *Catechismus attau Adjaran derri agamma Christaon. Bersalin derri bahassa Hollanda dalam Bahassa Maleya.* The Hague: widow of Hillebrant Jacobssz van Woue, 1623.
De Jong, Peter Y. "Early Reformed Missions in the East Indies." *Mid-America Journal of Theology* 6/1 (1990) 33-74.
End, Thomas van den. *Enam Belas Dokumen Dasar Calvinisme.* Jakarta: BPK Gunung Mulia, 2000.

Bibliography

———. *De Nederlandse Zendingsvereniging in West-Java, 1858–1963: Een bronnenpublicatie.* Raad voor de Zending der Ned. Herv. Kerk, Zending der Gereformeerde Kerken in Nederland, Gereformeerde Zendingsbond in de Ned. Herv. Kerk, 1991.

———. *Ragi Carita: Sejarah Gereja di Indonesia.* 2 vols. Jakarta: BPK Gunung Mulia, 1999.

———. *Sumber-Sumber Zending tentang Sejarah Gereja Toraja, 1901–1961.* Jakarta: BPK Gunung Mulia, 1994.

———. *Sumber-Sumber Zending tentang Sejarah Gereja Kristen Sumba, 1859–1972.* Jakarta: BPK Gunung Mulia, 1996.

Engelberts, Willem Jodocus Matthias. *Willem Teellinck.* Amsterdam: Scheffer, 1898.

Gaastra, F. "Introduction." In *The Archives of the Dutch East India Company (VOC) and the Local Institutions in Batavia (Jakarta),* edited by G. L. Balk, F. van Dijk, and D. J. Kortland, 13–207. Leiden: Brill, 2007.

———. "The Organization of the VOC." In *The Archives of the Dutch East India Company (VOC) and the Local Institutions in Batavia (Jakarta),* edited by G. L. Balk, F. van Dijk, and D. J. Kortland, 13–60. Leiden: Brill, 2007.

Gepken-Jager, Ella. "Verenigde Oost-Indische Compagnie (VOC)." In *VOC 1602–2002: 400 Years of Company Law.* Edited by Ella Gepken-Jager, Gerard Van Solinge, and Levinus Timmerman. Deventer, Netherlands: Kluwer Legal, 2005.

Gereformeerde Kerken in Nederland. "Formulier om den Heiligen Doop aan de kinderen te bedienen." In *De Formulieren van eenigheid, het kort begrip der christelijke religie, de liturgie der Gereformeerde Kerken in Nederland en de Dordtsche Kerkenorde.* Leeuwarden: A. Jongbloed, n.d.

Hof, W. J. op 't. "De Nadere Reformatie in Zeeland: Een eerste schets." In *Rond de kerk in Zeeland,* edited by A. Wiggers et. al. Delft: Eburon, 1991.

Kajajan, Hendrik. *De Pro-Acta der Dordtsche Synode in 1618.* Rotterdam: De Vries, 1914.

Kelley, M. T. *A Life of Saint Francis Xavier: Based on Authentic Sources.* St. Louis: B. Herder, 1918.

Landwehr, John. *VOC: A Bibliography of Publications Relating to the Dutch East India Company, 1602–1800.* Utrecht: HES, 1991.

Loderus, Andries Lambert. *Maleische Woord-Boek Sameling.* Batavia: VOC, 1707.

Loon, Hendrik Willem van. *The Golden Book of the Dutch Navigators.* New York: The Century Co., 1916.

Marsden, William. *A Grammar of the Malayan Language with Introduction and Praxis.* London: Cox and Baylis, 1812.

Nagtegaal, Luc. *Riding the Dutch Tiger: The Dutch East India Company and the Northeast Coast of Java, 1680–1743.* Translated by Beverley Jackson. Leiden: KITLV, 1996.

Niemeijer, Hendrik. *Batavia: Een koloniale samenleving in de zeventiende eeuw.* Amsterdam: Balans, 2005.

——— .*Calvinisme en koloniale stadscultuur: Batavia 1619–1725.* Amsterdam: Vrije Universiteit, 1996.

———. "Political Rivalry and Early Dutch Reformed Missions in Seventeenth-Century North Sulawesi." In *Missions and Missionaries,* edited by Peter N. Holtrop and Hugh McLeod, 32–49. Rochester, NY: Boydell, 2000.

Parthesius, Robert. *Dutch Ships in Tropical Waters: The Development of the Dutch East India Company Shipping Network in Asia 1595–1660.* Amsterdam: Amsterdam University Press, 2010.

Bibliography

Reseandt, W. Wijnaendts van. *De gezaghebbers der Oost-Indische Compagnieop hare buitencomptoiren in Azie*. Amsterdam: Liebaert, 1944.
Rogerio, Abraham. *Compendioso Exame dos Principaes Puntos de Religiaõ Christaõ Composto pello Philipe de Marnix, Senhor de Alegonde*. Amsterdam: Paulus Mathyz, 1688.
Ruyl, Albert. *Sovrat ABC, Akan meng ayd jer anack boudack sepercy deayd 'jern 'ja capada segala manusia Nassarany: daen berbagy sombahayang Christiaan*. Amsterdam: 1611.
———. *Sourat A, B, C, Jang bergouna banja capada anac bouda*. Amsterdam: Paulus Matthyz, 1682.
———. *Spieghel vande Maleysche Tale ende welcke sich die Indiaensche Jeucht Christlijk ende vermackelick kunnen oeffenendol eerliecke t'samenspraecken ende onderwijsinghen in de ware Godt-saligheyt tot voorstandt bande Christelijcke Religie. Met een Vocabularium van de Duytsche ende Maleysche Tale / dienstich voor alle liefhebbers der selver*. Amsterdam: Dirrick Pieters, 1612.
Ruyl, Albert Cornelisz. *Het Evangelie naar Mattheus*. Enkhuizen: Palenstein, 1629.
Schaff, Philip. *The Creeds of Christendom*. Vol. 3. Grand Rapids: Baker, 1983.
Schutte, Gerrit J. "Between Amsterdam and Batavia: Cape Society and the Calvinist Church under the Dutch East India Company." *Kronos* 25 (1998/1999) 17–49.
———, editor. *Het Indisch Sion: De Gereformeerde kerk onder de Verenigde Oost-Indische Compagnie*. Hilversum: Verloren, 2002.
———, editor. *State and Trade in the Indonesian Archipelago*. Leiden: KITLV, 1994.
Spiljardus, Josias. "Djalang ca Surga." Ms. Archief Classis Amsterdam SAA 379, 195, fol. 47–76.
Steenbrink, Karl. "The Arrival of Protestantism and the Consolidation of Christianity in the Moluccas 1605–1800." In *A History of Christianity in Indonesia*, edited by Jan Sihar Aritonang and Karel Steenbrink, 99–136. Leiden: Brill, 2008.
Taylor, Jean Gelman. *Indonesia: Peoples and Histories*. New Haven, CT: Yale University Press, 2003.
———. *Kehidupan Sosial di Batavia: Orang Eropa dan Eurasia di Hindia Timur*. Jakarta: Masup, 2009.
———. *The Social World of Batavia: Europeans and Eurasians in Colonial Indonesia*. Madison: University of Wisconsin Press, 2009.
Tuck, Patrick J. N. *The East India Company, 1600–1858*. New York: Routledge, 1998.
Uil, H. "De Nadere Reformatie en het onderwijs in Zeeland in de zeventiende eeuw." In *Documentatieblad Nadere Reformatie* 25/1 (2001) 1–18.
Valenteyn, François. *Ooud en Nieuw oost-Indien*. The Hague: H. C. Susan and C. Hzoon, 1856.
Wiltens, Caspar. *XIV. Maleysche Predicatien*. Amsterdam: 1648.
Wiltens, Caspar, and Sebastian Danckaerts. *Vocabularium, ofte Woordt-Boeck Naer Ordre van den Alphabet int't Duytsch-Maleysch ende Maleysch-Duytsch*. S'Gravenhage: Weduwe van Hillerbrant Jacobssz, 1623.
———. *Kitab Bacattahan daulo Malaio commedien Holando*. S'Gravenhage, 1623.

www.ingramcontent.com/pod-product-compliance
Lightning Source LLC
Chambersburg PA
CBHW051938160426
43198CB00013B/2198